"Parallel life"

"Parallel life"

ANTINANA MIZU

authorHOUSE®

AuthorHouse™ UK
1663 Liberty Drive
Bloomington, IN 47403 USA
www.authorhouse.co.uk
Phone: 0800.197.4150

Published by AuthorHouse 07/24/2015

ISBN: 978-1-5049-4207-2 (sc)
ISBN: 978-1-5049-4206-5 (hc)
ISBN: 978-1-5049-4208-9 (e)

Print information available on the last page.

I dedicate this book to my parents and my grand father who believe in my talent and support me with love and passion, to my children Denis and Emma the most precious trophy that live award me with. I love you and to you my loving husband with all my heart and eternal love.

A Parallel Life

In the darkness of the night, the lights of Las Vegas seemed like stars thrown out here and there in the transparent sky. I simply love all these bright lights, and I like to stare at them as if they were some kind of shiny toy.

I had been to the USA, but I hadn't seen Las Vegas before. On the surface, it seemed to be a fluorescent city. I knew there was some underground life here, but now I'm happy and I am not going to change the light into the darkness. Not anymore.

In the day light, the city seemed to lose its luster and luxury. It became slightly gray and I was part of it. Cosmin too.

Among the heavy curtains of time, after almost 25 years of absence, we would finally meet again. He offers a part of his soul, already filled with love, to nobody else but me.

My first night in Las Vegas, I wore a flowy black dress and black, shiny sandals. They were very comfortable and I could walk along the streets with no problem. I wanted to cross these streets and I wanted to feel them with all my heart. My pulse was excited and the blood accelerated in my veins. I felt no fatigue though I had traveled on long flights with a stopover in London for 9 hours. Over all, I knew I was a winner.

Now I was counting the seconds until I could smell his cologne as my lover would take me in his arms. Suddenly, the airport seemed too crowded.I was so nervous that I thought I would collapse there.

I couldn't see him yet, but I knew he hadn't changed very much since I had seen him last. I had the feeling that I would meet the same young man full of exuberance, hopes and dreams.In the crowd I finally saw him standing quietly, smiling warmly at me.

He was wearing faded jeans, a long sleeve red shirt, and on his head a brown cowboy hat. He was so handsome! The most handsome man in the world. And now he was all mine. I felt goose bumps on my skin as he walked towards me. My heart started pounding like a drum ready to beat through my chest. Although I was wearing a thin dress, I was so warm. I really don't know how I got into his arms. I only knew that I felt the softness of his lips on my lips. I felt like I had finally woken up from a long forgotten dream.

"Hey" he said and then he kissed me. "Welcome back to the Promised Land. Welcome back into my arms that have waited for you for so many years."

My eyes softened and it was like all the words got stuck somewhere in the depths of my inner being. I didn't know what to say and how to express my happiness. It was so intense. Yes, I was happy and suddenly I couldn't think properly. I couldn't remember when it was last that I had been so happy. He took my hand and led me outside to his red, used car. It seemed that all the stars were dancing in the sky for me and inside me. That's how I saw Las Vegas – full of light and wonder.

We went to his small apartment. It was sparsely furnished and smelled again of that specific scent of my man. A masculine fragrance. I was already dreaming of the beautiful nights that I would spend with him. I was going to live for REAL this time.

Bucharest, few months earlier

The old man was wearing a black cotton shirt and some striped, brown pajama pants. He woresoft, dark red slippers on his feet. His hair needed to be cut. I looked at him with compassion. Here, in this place, it smelled like death. I clenched my fists as I watched him.

His eyes seemed glasslike. He looked beyond the windows with that far away look. His face was gray, and through his open mouth trickled a few drops of saliva. For a few moments, the silence was heavier than eternity but then I heard his hoarse, dry cough. An endless cough, like a broken tractor that clanks and clatters.

I went to him and I gave him water. He took a breath, he choked and he coughed again.

"Should I call the nurse?" I asked, saddened at the desolate sight. A pitiful sight at the boundary between life and death. The thread of life so simply broken. I was a poor mortal too. I knew that I had no power to do anything.

The old man nodded. I knew I had to get the nurse immediately. I ran down the hall calling for the woman who was on duty that day.

"He's dying, he's dying ... er ... the old man… I think," I stammered. My whole being was full of fear. The nurse, whose name was Elena, looked calm yet slightly annoyed. I couldn't understand why.

"He's not dying now" she said as she took from a drawer a brown, little bottle with white cap and a little spoon. She passed by me calm, cold and collected. A faint soft smile hung on the corners of her mouth. She gave the old man two teaspoons of syrup, and then she left. I waited for her in the hallway. She took my hand and she looked me straight in the eye. "You see, you know this very well. People are coming here to say goodbye to life. They are coming here to die, OK? There is no need to tell you something you already know."

The hospital was in Voluntari, a small town near Bucharest. The grounds were beautifully landscaped with flowers. I called them "flowers of the death." Could flowers bring death for real? I remembered something I dreamt one night while I watched my father sleep. Some red and pink flowers were in a glass vase. Suddenly from the vase, gray smoke was rising that increasingly blackened the air and overtook everyone in the hospital. The smoke seeped into the air as it abducted the souls of the sick. With an obscure grimace, it passed with all of them into the other world. I woke up drenched in sweat. I heard my father's cough. This time it seemed like a tiger's roar in the Amazon rainforest.

When I saw that he was still asleep, I covered him with a thick blanket up to his chin. I left the hospital room, I went to the bathroom and I cried there with all my heart for about 10 minutes.

I was waiting my father to die. He had liver cancer and in February he would be 79 years old. Although you could say that he was old, he had been a strong man all his life. Struggling hard with misfortune, making a friend from his misery and trying to find his peace. He was afraid that the pain would prick his soul unto death. But he escaped. This time. The suffering had scarred his life. Life only occasionally gave him small joys and pauses. For example, the birth of my son, Dennis was such a blessing to him. I knew for sure that for Dennis, if it were needed, he would give his life with no regrets.

He gave to my son a pure and unconditional love. He blessed us with kindness and gentleness. And my child became to my father all he wanted most in the world.

*   *   *

I was looking out the window as twilight faded away leaving the room to a dark deep night without stars. I wanted to see the stars appearing in the sky as to somehow lighten my heart and soul. But my soul was gray and the stars didn't shine. Too many clouds, too much bitterness on Earth.

I wanted to cry. I felt a damn lump in my throat, but my tears had dried long ago.

My father continued to sleep. The cancer made its way in making it look like something had eaten his body. I was praying every minute, every hour, every night that my father's suffering would end. The hope in a miracle was all gone and wasted.

I looked at the big clock on the wall. It was midnight. I wasn't sleepy and I felt fatigue infiltrating into my body. I rejected it fiercely. I didn't want to crash now. I wanted to stay beside my father, picking up the scent of his breath, until the last one.

I hadn't eaten anything all day long. I wasn't hungry. I just wanted water. A lot of water to wash my body and soul from the rotten air, smelling like death.

I heard a faint sound and I turned back to my father. The old man next to my father's bed was making some monstrous sounds. I called them "sounds of death".

My dad had awoken. His eyelids were loose and his eyes were bloodshot."Father," I mumbled and I sat down on his bed beside him."Laura ... uh ... Laura ... I wan tsome water, please. I took a glass full of water on the bedside table and gave it to him. I helped him drink it. He drank greedily, knowing perhaps that his time was running out and there were only a few days or a few moments left.

"Oh", he said satisfied. "I was so thirsty! I felt like my soul was burning." "Yes, father," I said, forcing a tortured smile. "Do you want an apple or an orange?" Unlike the old man who occupied the next bed, my father's saliva hadn't trickled from the corners of the lips. I was happy for this. I felt like his time had not yet come. Dad nodded. He wanted to sit up so I helped him. I put the pillow under his back so he could sit more comfortably despite his pain.

"Is it morning already, Laura?" "No Dad, it's midnight and the wind is blowing hard. Why don't you sleep?" My father smiled. His eyes glittered in the dim light of lamps.

"I feel like I have slept forever. But you know, all I want is to sleep more. I feel like I am living in a different world with many lights and shadows. I have no dreams, Laura. Simply as that, I have no more dreams. Or maybe I confuse dreams with the reality. I don't know my dear, my world has turned upside down. However, I accept this world that reeks of helplessness. I accept it because I'm weak. What do you want? You want me to shout out loud that it's not right?"

I took his warm hand in my hand. "Whatever you say, father." Then I looked out of the window and I smiled sadly. "Tomorrow I think the sun will rise" I said.

"If the sun rises, will you take me outside? I will ask Him to send me a sunshine."

"A ray of hope, daddy?" I laughed. "You know... hope dies last..."

Dad sighed, "Yes, it's true, but ultimately, after a long struggle, hope dies."

*   *   *

My father struggled for 3 months in the hospital. He didn't suffer much because the doctors gave him medication to fight the pain. Ultimately, the cancer crushed his weak, emaciated body like a worm in a red healthy apple.

It was in December and the snow still hadn't arrived in Bucharest. In the rest of the country were snow storms, but we were avoided, thank God. It would have been more difficult for me had the winter been bad as I walked daily to public transportation. I would have lost hours of my father's life, away from him, trapped in buses full of people full of other problems. There were nights when I slept at my mother-in-law's home so I could spend my days in the hospital near my father. Sometimes when I heard his tough and hard breath and I saw his eyelids tightly glued, and his breathing becoming weaker, I felt I had to stay beside him no matter what.

There were three beds in the room. One was occupied by my father, the second one was given to the old man with gray hair and in the third one I would rest myself whenever I needed. I was always waiting for tomorrow with all its anticipation and hopes, but I knew it was just a matter of a few days and the Death would come with a hissly grin and take dad away from me with no mercy.

When the time came, I sold my car to have funds to bury my father. In Romania it is even hard to die, but there is no point to write now about the economy, because I'm not good at it. I know that the majority of people work in vain, writhing in terrible poverty. This is the daily life in my country.

* * *

One morning, my father coughed so loudly that he scared the old man next to him who muttered some kind of mean whisper: "You will die soon," which fortunately, wasn't heard by my father. I looked at the old man very quickly and frowned. He spoke the truth, but that hurt me terribly.

"Dad, what is it?"

My dad waited to stop coughing and he said softly: "I feel like I'm drowning. These damn cigarettes... they turned my entire life into ash."

"Yes Dad. I always told you to leave them for good and you would fire back at me. Thinking that all I wanted was bad for you and the good things were all in your hands and you knew better. What do you think now, huh? Can you see the real face of things?"

I poured tea from a bottle that was brought by my aunt. He took the cup and he drank it eagerly."Do you like it? Was it good?" I asked.

"What an irony! I'm drinking tea, hehe... I think it would have been better if it had been a cold beer."

I laughed softly, trying to create a relaxed atmosphere. "A cold beer ... with all pleasure sir, but when we get out of here."

He said, "The only way I will be leaving here is in a casket. I will place myself nicely into eternity."

The tears I had held back finally swam in my eyes. "Don't say that Dad."

"It's just stupid words spoken by a foolish old man, dear." he said.

It was almost dark. Street lights pierced the darkness one by one, and the hospital was quiet and frightening like a gothic painting. I looked out of the window and I sighed deeply, then I heard my dad, "Go home, Laura. You need to rest." I turned to him perplexed. I thought he was already sleeping but he was sitting there watching me.

"And it will go down every day for the rest of our lives." I found myself speaking. Then I sat down beside him. "How are you, Dad?"

"As a newborn child," he smiled. "I sleep a lot!"

"You need it to recover. Your body is weak."

"Strange, he said. I have no pain. Why do they still keep me here?"

"*That's your last stop*," a thought shouted at me.

That night I went home.

*   *   *

December 1st - National Day of Romania. Dad turned on the TV. It was only me and him in the room. The old man who shared the room died two nights before.

My mother died in my arms, also by cancer. I was only 19. I think death itself is just a passage to another world. I don't think this reality is over just like that. God's ways are not so simple and clear, or maybe they are simple, it's just us who complicate everything. However, my father told me that night: "Do you know, Laura, that the old man had cancer?"

I grimaced trying to make it look like a smile. I nodded instinctively. My dry lips refused to utter a word. On television, a military parade starting from the Arc of Triomphe was on.My father seemed fascinated by theparade with all the uniformed soldiers walking in unison. With bloodshot eyes and parted lips, which formed a faded smile, the man who had made the impossible possible for me was so close to saying goodbye to life. For me though, he wasn't going to die. Never ever. I had then a strange revelation. I imagined my dad dragging his days into eternity and when my time arrived, he would be the one takes me up to Heaven. But in that moment, I wanted to go with him wherever Death wanted to take him. I wanted to pass through that invisible gate into eternity. But another powerful thought came into my mind that removed this strange desire. *"You have two children who need you. You'll pass through the gate but not now, another day, another day ... another day."*

On December 1st, Dad enjoyed life again. Some friends came to visit him and they brought hot soup, fresh fruit and sweets. They talked about their youth all day long. My father wasn't tired and he didn't sleep.

On that day, I also had in my heart one thing I forgotten the feeling of. How it felt to be happy.

* * *

Dennis, my 18 years old son, visited my father in the hospital a couple of times. He was young and sickened by the idea of his grandfather's death. He didn'twant to come again into that grey hospital full of sick people.

"You know, Mom, I don't want to see how life is draining slowly from him, like the sand from an hourglass. I want to remember him like the man who did everything for me. He suffered everytime I had a cold and even for all the scratches I had. He loved me unconditionally."

My childs eyes filled with tears and his whole body was shaking. I couldn't bear to see him in pain. "Don't come dear," I said.

"But he wants to see me," Dennis sighed wiping his tears with the back of his sleeve.

"It doesn't matter. You've made his life so beautiful from the moment you were born. This is undeniable. Death is not a very pleasant thing to see, and you're too young to suffer. Go to school and occupy your mind with your books. Do what I say and leave this trouble on my shoulders. Go! Go! I love you, darling!"

On the evening of December 8th, my father started to make some terrible noises. He rolled his eyes and talked to himself. It is said that when this happens, the dying one is actually talking to the dead people. I don't know what to say about that, but Dad started waving his hands around as he talked with invisible things or creatures, like somebody else or something else was in the room. He was talking with no pause, but I didn't understand much. I cried desperately and I called the doctor.

"It's his last night'" said the doctor, with an annoying tranquility.

I wasn't able to say anything because I was crying continuously. My daddy, my sweet gentle daddy. He went to the other world, leaving us behind in this cruel world.

"Why father, why?" I sighed painfully.

I sat beside him, listening to his secret words and seeing his furious gestures. Maybe he wanted to clear the clouds of death coming, grinning and showing his deadly scythe. Maybe he just wanted to taste one more piece of life quietly, without so much struggle. But he was fighting, fighting, fighting. I asked him some questions, but he refused to answer.

On December 9th, on a cold, frosty, winter morning, my father said goodbye to the world.

*   *   *

I buried my father the next day and many people came to his funeral. Maybe the angels in heaven greeted him too. I like to think so.

I cried a lot. Dennis cried too. We remained embraced in pain for hours and hours. We felt a deep loneliness surrounding us.

*   *   *

One month later, I left Romania for Las Vegas. There I would try to live my life like I never had before. I left in late January. And finally in

Romania, winter really settled in. Snow had been projected all over the country. It arrived in Bucharest too. But in Las Vegas, the sun shone. I hoped that the same rays would dance that great dance of joy inside my soul, still trapped in pain.

*   *   *

Bucharest, August, 1974

On that summer morning, the sun already shone high in the sky, smiling to the whole world. I looked out the window through the pulled curtains and I saw my mother hanging out the washed clothes with one hand–the left one, because the right one had been operated on five years ago and she hardly could move her fingers. Yet, she still had the power to care of us and comfort us in the best possible way. Dad was at work and my grandfather was concentrating on reading a book about how communism had taken over Romania. My grandfather was a revolutionary man. He had spent 20 years in the U.S. and he knew how to handle the real life.

In Romania, everything was bursting at the seams. Unfortunately, this was only the beginning. People's lives had taken an unpleasant turn under communism and its president, Ceausescu. I didn't know anything about it. Micky, my little sister muttered something in her sleep, opened her mouth, as if she wanted to say a word, but she closed it suddenly. She continued her sweet morning sleep. I went out barefoot and I called my mom.

"What is it, Laura?" she smiled knowing that today was the big day.

"Mommy," I cried filled with such joy. I went to her and I hugged her legs. "Today, today ... I'm going."

"I know, I know Laura, we are going to the gym today."

"Yes Mom," and I hugged her again happy as a child can be.

Mom took me in her arms as best as she could with her healthy hand and she kissed me on my cheeks.

"Come on, go and wash your face! I'll set the table immediately. Did your sister wake up?"

"No, Micky is snoring and the windows are shaking."

My mother laughed lightly.

"Oh, don't exaggerate, my dear!"

My sister was one year younger than me and we understood each other perfectly. I said a cheerful "good morning" to my grandfather and I kissed him on the cheek. The old man smiled back to me with an undisguised love. I knew I was the favorite of all his grandchildren. I felt this every day as much as my soul could feel at that age.

I went into the bathroom and I pulled off my teddy bear pajamas. I turned on the shower, I rubbed my head with shampoo then I used it to wash my body.

Today I was supposed to be the cleanest and the most beautiful girl in the world. My mother prepared my pink fluffy dress with large ruffles. Oh boy, I loved pink so much! Even pink candies and of course pink cream cakes that my father would bring home.

Mother prepared the breakfast: boiled eggs, ham, butter and milk. I ate it all with my mother and grandfather because Micky was still sleeping. She would remain at home with Grandpa.

*   *   *

"Dinamo" club was at some distance from where I lived. We went by bus then we took a tram to Stephan the Great station. There was a huge park that I liked to admire and walk in.

"Do you like it?" my mother asked me.

I was simply enchanted by the landscape in front of me. A football stadium (that I've seen on TV), a pool with blue water (actually, the basin was blue, but I didn't realize it then) and many trees and flowers of different colors. There were many rooms where children practiced all kind of sports, but I wanted to see the gym room so much.

"Yes, yes and yes," I said to mother, jumping from one foot to another at a dizzying pace.

*   *   *

The gym seemed enormous to me. The gym was identical to that where Nadia Comaneci excelled in Montreal. What do they call her? "Montreal Goddess." A rising gymnast, who wasn't afraid to dream and feel the glory. From the first moment I saw her, I would dream of her and I didn't want my sweet dream falling apart.

I remember one night dreaming of Nadia again. She was smiling at me with her bright smile and she stretched out a hand and helped me climb on the podium. "Right beside you, Nadia" I whispered with softly voice, almost crying.

"Yes, right beside me."

"Hello, Laura," a man's voice woke me up from my daydream.

I was smiling. There, among my own dreams, I was happy. I looked at the man and I didn't know what to say. I was dizzy.

"Laura, he will be your coach. Mr. Florin Stefanescu," said my mother, trying to get my attention.

The smile widened on his face.

"Dearest, Laura, I am so glad you like this sport."

I stretched my little fragile hand that showed its blue tiny veins.

"I like to climb on the bars and sometimes I make tumbles," I laughed. "I know how to "wheel" and I can do "the bridge" like a real gymnast. I'm not going to the kindergarten yet but after this year, I'll go to school.

I was kind of verbose that day. I simply couldn't stop talking. Maybe I wanted to calm some of the emotions that overwhelmed me. But that day is in my memory as one of the most important days of my life. It was the day when I came into the world that I dreamed about for so many days and nights, like the gym world was something sacred to me. It was and will be until the end.

Starting that day for about one year, I trained almost every day. We had contests and although I was quite little, I managed to win in competions countless times. I worked hard and even when Mr. Stefanescu raised his voice at me, I held him close to my heart. I knew that he wished all the best for me. I was getting used to the thought that I'd be a huge gymnast.

My grandfather took me every day to the gym and, although he was approaching 80 years old, he had the vitality and the quick, fresh mind of a young man. He read books in English. He loved life as many young people maybe don't. He ventured daily from home to gym and gym to home, only because he believed in me. Sometimes my mother took me to the gym. I worked so hard that my palms became calloused, but I never complained. It was my decision to go on no matter what. The dream of being on the podium alongside Nadia was sketched into my brain. The vivid picture of that dream washed away any physical or psychological pain. I was trying to create a happy world for me, even if the childhood games remained just a sweet remembrance for me.

One year later I started school. My grandfather and my mother were taking me to school, then to gym. In those days, all the gyms had the option to live and reside in the club, as a type of internship. There we would eat, shower, do homework, rest awhile (though I still had enough energy), and then continue my journey training. When I was taught a new exercise, I would repeat it until exhaustion. I was a frail girl but I followed my dream. It had to become reality, my young mind reiterated this to my body. I was very determined. No matter how many wounds I had on my hands, no matter how many broken bones, I knew one thing: I had to struggle mightily to become a winner.

And I will be a champion.

*   *   *

One evening, my father came home from his work with a pink, huge cake and several bottles of beer. He worked at a coffee shop, and my sister, Micky and I enjoyed all the goodies in the world. We had a very sweet childhood. I was lucky that I didn't gain weight, otherwise goodbye dreams, goodbye gym.

At that time, I also had a cousin who was taken to the gym by her mother, but she didn't like it as much as I did. She would sneak out of the room and would hide in the bushes.

"I simply don't like it, Laura! I just want to study, I hate sports!"

"Then, why are you going?" I asked her.

Her eyes filled with tears, and I put a hand on her shoulder affectionately.

"Because Mom wants it. And I love Mom. I want her to be happy."

"Don't go, Mirela. I'll talk to Grandpa about this."

My grandfather again performed a miracle by convincing his daughter, Mirela's mother, to leave her daughter alone and let her study as she wanted. But that was my grandfather, he performed miracles every day, small miracles.

As soon as my father came into the house, my sister and I embraced him and we kissed him on both cheeks.

"What are you doing Dad? How was your day?"

"I brought you this wonderful cake and something to drink for me and for Grandpa."

We both jumped around from one leg to the other. Is there a child in the world who doesn't like sweets?

"But do you know why I brought you cake?" (He usually came with cupcakes and cookies).

"It's somebody's birthday father!" said Micky.

"No, but it's a special day for Laura and that makes the day special for all of us. We are united in joy and trouble. But today is a joyful day."

"A special day for me?" I asked.

"Tell me father, why is it special?" I chirped like a little bird.

"This week you will go to a competition in Germany."

My heart started to beat faster as my blood ran faster in my veins. I was about to travel for the first time to another country. My parents never traveled abroad.

* * *

After I came back from Germany, I fell in love with Cosmin. He was one year older than me. I remember doing a new exercise on uneven bars (my favorite gym apparatus) and during this exercise, I hit my left ankle. It immediately appeared as a swollen bruise like a rotten potato. The pain was excruciating and I began to cry silently. My cheeks were wet with tears, but I tried to ignore the pain. I gritted my teeth to support all the pain. Everyone was busy with their own problems and I felt like I was part of another universe. A universe of unhappy children.

My coach was busy with another girl and he didn't notice the suffering I was experiencing. But one boy saw me and he came to me. He was fragile too. And he had interrupted his exercise for me. He squatted down and touched my ankle. His fingers were soft as silk, which was very strange, because all the gymnasts had bruises on their palms. I watched him fingering my ankle and I thought for a moment that he was a kid with a big heart.

"It hurts, doesn't it?" he asked me.

Did I forget the pain? Did it disappear under his soft fingers? Or was I just a child dreaming a wonderful dream about love and glory?

"Does it hurt you?" he asked me again.

"Yep!," I whimpered, casting a faint sound from my throat.

I wiped my tears and I saw him looking at me slightly sad.

"I'm sorry! I'm going to tell the coach."

I was tempted to say no, but my ankle was throbbing. Mr. Stefanescu carried me in his arms and took me to the doctor's office and the boy followed.

"Can I come?" he asked the coach.

"Sure, Cosmin. You are a good team-player."

I saw his beautiful lips curve into a shy smile. Doctor Marin bandaged me. It hurt so much, but all I did was grit my teeth until I heard Cosmin's voice again.

"There is no need to keep the pain in you. If you want to yell or cry, just do it!"

I took a deep breath, then let it out slowly. For a second I thought that the pain had subsided. I yelled as he told me. After a few minutes, the pain lessened, but I still couldn't walk properly on my left leg. I felt however, some sort of peace seeing theboy with the silky voice and silky fingers. Mr. Stefanescu took me home in his small, purple car. Cosmin followed me with his eyes until I left the office and then the gym. As I left, I flashed him my sweetest smile.

*   *   *

I found out that Cosmin and I went to the same school. I was in second grade and he was in the fourth. In between classes, we met and talked about the gym. It was the most important thing that united us. We smiled often to each other and sometimes his fingers touched my hand by mistake. I observed that he also had calluses on his hands like I did, but I still felt like they were softer than ‚silk'.

Then we went together to boarding school. Older team mates called us "little lovers." Even the coaches called us "little lovers" but it was something very pure and innocent, a childish love.

*   *   *

I had competed at many national and international competitions with Cosmin. Two years had passed since we met each other and seemed ... no, we didn't seem, we really were two happy children. My Grandpa continued to bring me to the club, with a smile always hanging on the corners of his mouth. The best grandfather in the world. Every summer day he bought me ice cream, and in the winter, he had me drink hot lemon tea. I gathered him in my arms and I kissed him on his cheek.

"You're the best grandpa in the world. You know that, right? I would like to give you a star, I want you to be immortal."

And my grandfather answered:

"But I am immortal ... As long as you will be with me."

"Ok, ok, that's wonderfull," I said happy. "Aren't you tired of these roads?"

"No, never," giggled Grandpa.

*   *   *

Bucharest, an ordinary day

On that August day, the sun shone fiercely early in the morning. I woke up early because I had to go, as usual, to training. My mother accompanied me, because, after the gym classes, she wanted to go shopping with me. Micky and I needed a new dress. We were all going to a party that weekend.

The day was quiet, serene and very calm. From a distance, birds could be heard chirping joyfully. The smell of linden flowers invaded my nostrils as soon as I was out of the house. I breathed deeply and I felt the full plenitude of life. I smiled, grateful to be alive, and for the sun and the world.

My mom called for me to come eat some breakfast. My mother, grandfather and I ate. Micky, as usual, was sleeping at that hour. She was so lazy and I called her "lazy girl" whenever she annoyed me. Only when she had to go to school would she wake up early.

I ate and then I thanked God, with that specific tranquility only a child with clear conscience could have. And I was just a kid, right? And a kid should be happy and have a happy childhood.

I took a shower and I washed my hair. I had hair down to my shoulders and I already took care of it without help from my mother. Then I put on a dress with ruffles, the kind I liked. I didn't dry my hair. I liked the wind to brush it and dry it with its warm breeze.

A few minutes later I left home with my mother. We went to the bus stop across the street, waiting impatiently for the bus.

* * *

Micky was so proud because she looked like a bride from American movies, curly hair, along with her mother's lipstick on her girlish lips and high heels. She was cheerful, with a great big smile as she waved her hand to the boy at the other side of the road. He called her insistently.

"Come on! Come on, Micky! Come on!"

"Here I come! I'm comiiiing!"

Nobody saw the big truck that approached with ominous speed. The truck hit the little girl, killing her instantly. Blood began to flow in warm waves and pieces of her brain were scattered on the road.

And the day was quiet, serene and very calm.

* * *

As we returned home, our arms were loaded with shopping bags. Mom bought me a summer dress and silver sandals. Micky had the same clothes, only different colors. Usually, when we were very very little, mother would dress us alike, but now that I was almost 10, I wanted to be different. We weren't twins.

We were still on the bus when the mother noticed a crowd of people in our backyard. The bus stop was just near our house. She grabbed my hand forcefully and I looked at her worried.

"What is it, Mom?" I asked her.

"Laura, something has happened, why are so many peoplelooking in our backyard?"

There were men and women everywhere. I see them even now. Long crips faces.But I didn't see my grandfather or Micky. "Nothing happened, nothing bad happened," I mechanically repeated to myself. I felt a nervous tremor in my fingertips.

We got off the bus and we headed home. An old woman with snow-white hair saw us, she opened her mouth to say something, but the sound of her voice was melted in her throat. She held a withered hand to her mouth. She was very anxious. Then all of the sudden, the people turned to us as we entered the courtyard. Dad appeared with tears in his eyes, and I noticed that his lower lip trembled stronger than ever.

"Daddy?"

My breathing became labored, like a little rabbit that ran in front of its hunter. My father was crying and he said through tears:

"I'm sorry, Stela."

Then he embraced us with all his strength that remained. Mother became pale and she fell onto the asphalt heated by the sun.

$$* \quad * \quad *$$

It was like a nightmare, people appeared to be crooked and ugly with yellow, rotten teeth smiling at me. I could see their eyes and twisted mouths calling me "Laura! Lauraaaaa!" It suddenly became so dark and

I saw them as wandering shadows that appeared from nowhere. Then there was a powerful light. A light that blinded me as if the sun was mad at me.

"Mom? Where are you, Mother?"

"Dad? Where are you, Dad?"

"Grandpa, Micky, where are you?"

"In a world where you can't be for the moment," I heard my father's voice that echoed clearly in my mind, like torture.

"What do you want from me? I'll do anything to be with you."

I felt that I was in a bubble of water and I wondered how the bubble was so strong and not breaking. I floated through the air like a feather and I couldn't find anybalance. I was floating somewhere between heaven and earth, full of fear. So it seemed to me then. Now I know that the fear can be overcome by the power of prayer and believing in God.

But then, in that terrible day, I saw people approaching my bubble ball ready to push me and break my nest. I looked at them surprised. All the figures were distorted and they had the features of somer epulsive monsters."Moooom!" I cried.

I heard a heartbreaking scream come out of my lungs. An inhuman yell.

I cried again, but my screams melted into nothingness. I could also hear faint sobs of another person tortured by his own pain. Then shouts, anxiety, dread. I began to cry loudly only because I couldn't stand the mystery. I knew something bad had happened but nobody wanted to tell me what.

I left my protective bubble, perhaps it had broken. We were walking now with shuffling steps among people who put their hands on my shoulder, as if they wanted to give me affection. In one corner of the courtyard, the one covered with grape-vines, I saw my grandfather. He came to me with eyes swimming in tears. People stepped aside, making room for my grandfather to pass. Although I was aware that he was coming to me, I felt like he stood there and he was further from me than ever. Eventually I lost patience and I ran towards him, but my legs felt like I was paralyzed.

After a while, I felt Grandpa take me in his arms. Over his shoulder, I saw the shopping bags our new dresses were in. The sandals had fallen outside the boxes right there on the street.

My grandfather took me into the house, where there was no one but us. He asked me to sit beside him on the fluffy green couch. I watched him with the greatest love in the world, but also with fear. A deep unknown fear, the fear grew when I saw all those people and now it had reached its climax. I was afraid of what he would tell me.

"What's with all these people, Grandpa? What's happening in our backyard? It's suffocating, really."

Grandpa took a deep breath, and then exhaled the air from his lungs in a long sigh. He took my hand and he squeezed it gently. He looked me straight in the eyes.

"What is it, Grandpa?"

My heart jumped in my chest. I barely had the courage to ask him anything more. Grandfather began to speak to me with a very sad voice.

"Laura, you know how much grandpa loves you, right?"

I nodded a silent yes.

"From the earth to the heavens and beyond. You are a big girl now. I mean, you are grown up, right?"

I shook my head again, although I was just a kid who is just discovering life. And now it looks like I was about to discover death.

I exploded like I was a time bomb that couldn'twait to explode.

"What is it, Grandpa? What's all this nonsense? I want to know what has happened to us!"

I started to cry because no one said anything to me.

"The sun is down, Grandpa," I said at one point.

Tears began to flow from his eyes.

"Yes, Laura, for us the sun is down."

"But it will rise again, right?"

"Maybe, someday. For sure it will rise for you, a big shiny great star, and it will smile down to you. Laura, listen to me," he said after a short pause, during which he kissed my hand. "Grandpa loves you a lot and he doesn't want you to suffer. But I have to say something that will make you suffer. You have to suffer, it's normal, and I just hope tha tsomeday you'll get over it."

"What happened? Tell me."

"Micky ... you know, our little Micky ... your sister ... she had an accident. Laura, you have to be strong, my dear."

"Mom ... Where's Mom?" I asked.

I remembered that my mother had fallen earlier in the yard. I couldn't see her anywhere and I was worried. If my mother had fallen unconscious in the yard, then it really would be a tragedy. But still I couldn't believe in a tragedy, especially at the age I couldn't understand it.

"Micky is ok, right? She had an accident, but she'll be fine. If she hit her head, she can be sewn, and that's it. If she broke a leg or a hand, it will be placed in a cast and she'll be healed, right Grandpa? I will give her autographs on her cast and I will bring all her friends to the hospital to do the same. We'll have a great time," and I began to laugh hysterically.

My grandfather squeezed my arm tightly, letting me know quietly that I talked of nonsense.

"Laura ... your sister died."

He said it quickly. It had to be a joke. It couldn't be any other way.

"Come on, Grandpa, it's a joke. Micky is in the hospital and she will be fine. Mom and Dad are there to protect her."

"Come on, Grandpa, let's go outside and chase away those people with ugly faces."

Grandpa realized that I was in shock. Weeping, he tried to make me accept the cruel reality.

"Come on, Grandpa, let's get these people out of our yard then let's go to the hospital to see Micky. I want to say hello to her if she's awake. And I want to tell her that if she has a cast, I will bring all her friends to put autographs on it. We will laugh together as always. I'm sorry that I told her so many times that she was restless. She's not. She's sweet, and delicate, and so beautiful."

Grandpa stood up. His face seemed carved in stone. His features had become tougher and tougher.

"Don't you understand, Laura?" he raised his voice. "Micky died. Now she is among angels."

"An angel among angels," I mumbled to myself feeling suddenly wasted and tired.

I still couldn't accept it. *"Maybe Grandpa is playing with me a twisted game"*

"Maybe stars will not fall"

"Maybe life does not end"

"Maybe the sun won't go down"

"My sweet little sister is an angel now? Why? What could she have been done to deserve this? Good things or bad things? Did she play more than she should? Or less?"

*   *   *

When Micky was brought home from the morgue, I realized what it meant to be "an angel among angels." She had a huge wound on her head. I presumed that the doctors washed the blood away because I didn't see a drop of it. Her forehead, particulary on the left side, was flattened by the damn truck that hit her. I stood beside her casket plagued by sad thoughts.

I sat beside her, kissing her smashed forehead and her cold hands. I was talking to her as if she were alive. I wanted so much to have my sister back. Vivacious and sometimes nasty, answering me bluntly, as she did when I bothered her.

"Laura, you'll be somebody one day. A great gymnast. And I will applaud you from my chair, with our mother and our grandfather. We will weep with happiness when you are on the podium and we will open a bottle of champagne, in your honor."

"Micky, will you open a bottle of champagne in heaven in my honor?" I thought to myself aloud.

Several people attending the vigil looked at me sympathetically. I wept beside her as relatives appeared. A sea of tears flowed down my cheeks. I was exhausted from crying. I promised to talk to my sister every day and try to smile again, even if I didn't succeed with more than a pathetic grimace.

* * *

My mother fainted two or three times. A nurse at the clinic was present and gave her intravenous calcium. She didn't want painkillers, because, she said, they were ravaging her soul wrecked with pain. She wanted to cry out loud in her pain, screaming and yelling, like a hungry wolf in the forest. She wanted to move mountains and give life back to her child.

She didn't mind at all that the crowd saw her collapsed and in a pitiful state. Only a mother who lost her child could understand her pain.

* * *

After Micky was buried (her full name was Michaela), I felt a huge void in my heart. All my feeling shad disappeared and all that was left was emptiness. Every time I looked at my mother, I saw her speeking in a whisper to someone invisible. I thought that the sun will no longer rise for us.

My mother wept for about one year like a sinister ritual, becoming ordinary. All of her crying darkened my soul. One day she asked to take me to the gym, trying to leave the past behind.

I tried to do whatever was possible to bring a smile to my mother's face. I trained the best I could and waited to be praised by my coach, Mr. Stefanescu. One day I even said to him: "Please, coach, tell my mother whenever I am doing well. She'll be pleased and she will maybe even smile. Maybe I'm asking too much from you, but I really want my mom to be able to enjoy life again. She swims in a powder keg that could explode at any moment. Do this for me, please!" Then I started to cry with sadly resigned tears.

Coach embraced me like a father and he said: "You know, Laura, people go to Heaven. There's another world and I think it is a better world than the one here. Micky went too early into that world and you are too young to carry this burden on your frail shoulders. You are just a child and happiness should wait for you around every corner. I will tell your mom about your performance. And some day she will smile again."

A month after my sister's death, I went to a competition in Hungary. My father and my grand father encouraged me but my mother remained cold as ice, shrouded in her black cloak. She didn't have the strength to shake her blackness. Maybe, I thought, there was no way. It was too early to ask the impossible and bring her into my world where sacrifices demanded their reward.

* * *

I was working hard at the gym, wanting to give my best. My talents and abilities helped me a lot. Cosmin was always beside me, showing me sincere affection. We were kids, and our feelings pure as white lilies that open in the morning.

And the time came when my mother came to my competitions. I kissed her cheeks and I tried to make her see the stars in my life. Her black, mourning silhouette watched the crowd that would applaud me every time I performed on uneven bars. I smiled at her with my white teethwatching her beyond the crowds. "Maybe I can see her," I wished to myself. "Maybe she is proud of me." But I had no certainty.

She would kiss me every night before I would fall asleep and because it was autumn, she covered me with a thick blanket. She would smile at me but I knew that her smile wasn't like it used to be. "She will never be the same," I thought, "and her voice will remain in silence forever." I didn't dare to ask her about my sister. I was afraid that I would create a catastrophe in a still bleeding heart. At the same time, I knew that she needed me. She stroked my hair and my forehead:

"Do not ever leave me, Laura!" she said.

My eyes swam in tears:

"Mom ... you know ... I have competitions, but I will never leave you."

"I'm proud of you, my girl. I think I'll touch the stars through you. My darling, you have sparkles in your life and if you are happy, I'm happy too. I'll try to see the light that you are looking for." (I knew what she meant).

Then she stood up and she looked out of the window. I will never forget her sad silhouette, bow down like all the worries of the world were carried on her shoulders.

"Mom?"

She turned to me and she smiled broadly, a smile that made me happy."What is it, Laura?"

"Tonight I will sleep happy, thinking of you and I will dream of you. In my dreams you will be happy. You know Mom, I'll be a winner. And you'll be even more proud of me."

Mom kissed me on the forehead again and she covered me with the blanket up to my chin."Sleep well! God be with you!"

She walked out and turned off the light. She left the room as if she walked on air. I was sure that my mom made an ally out of her suffering, and the mere thought made me suffer more.

I fell asleep and I dreamed of my mother as I had wanted. I was somewhere in the universe, a night with many stars, and my mother rode the banana shaped moon. She wore a white dress that reached to her ankles. I was hanging from a star and I clearly heard her song that she wa singing with such an endearing voice.

"To whom is my mom singing?" I wondered.

Then I saw the baby in her arms wrapped in white diapers. I realized, that was Micky. Mama was singing too sweet and the baby in her arms couldn't be anybody but my sister. Her voice was resounding like an echo in the Universe. I was clinging to a star, my hand supporting my chin and I listened spellbound by my mother's sad voice. When I opened my eyes in the middle of the night, her voice still reverberated in my ears, like a distant, sweet and sorrowful echo.

It was dark in my room. I had slept only two or three hours when my thoughts began to race in my head. I thought of Micky when we were little.We had gone into the green sea, full of algae. Our joyful voices mingled with the murmur of the crowd buzzing at the beach and the sound of the waves. We were so happy and we made our parents happy just because we existed. They watched us from their white sheets and we simply bathed in their smiles.

Then I thought about Cosmin and our pure childish love. I sincerely hoped that the feeling was mutual. Of course my friend shared the same feelings. His tender gestures, slightly clumsy (he was only 11 years old).

I sifted through the memories until dawn. I couldn't close my eyes. I wasn't used to sleeping alone and my sleep didn't want to come. I got up at five in the morning. All of my dearests were still sleeping and the house was in a deep silence.

I went out into the yard and the cool air of autumn shook me. I loved the cool freshness, feeling it down into my lungs as it purified them. I stayed out about 10 minutes then I went back into the house. I lit the lamp and I read a poem that I had to memorize for school. Although I only slept for a short period of time, I felt as fresh as bread out from the oven. I was serene, and my actions followed their usual path. School, pension, gym.

"I must do my best," I said with my heart full of devotion.

That day my grandfather took me to school and in the afternoon it was my mom's turn to take me home. But she wanted to go to the cemetery to talk to Micky. Yes, just to talk. Inside perhaps, the howling had to be repressed little by little.

"Mom, you aren't coming with me?" I asked her while she poured hot milk into my cup.

She smiled sadly. "Today I want to unchain my pain, Laura. I want to remove some of the venom that covers my heart."

"Will you cry, Mom?"

"If the tears come, yes, darling, I will cry. I want to talk to your sister, listen to her pain and her joy and I want to tell her about your achievements. I'll ask her to forgive me every time I feel joy when you smile and you are happy." Then she put down the kettle and she continued: "Oh, I am so foolish! Of course she enjoys it. There is no other way. She was a little girl with a big heart."

In my mother's eyes weren't tears, only a slight shadow of sadness. And when she spoke, she had a bitter, weak smile in corners of her mouth.

I felt like she had resigned. She cried so much that her tears had dried up inside her.

*   *   *

Two years later, in the cold month of January, my coach, Stefanescu came to me while I was repeating an exercise.

"Stop it, Laura. I want to talk to you. There is somthing I need you and your parents to know,"

I was nervous and had butterflies in my stomach. I was afraid that I wasn't good enough for his standards and I couldn't live up to his expectations. Although at the national examinations I did pretty well I thought.

"Have I done something bad?" I stammered, like a man awaiting the verdict: guilty or not guilty.

"What do you mean by "bad" Laura?"

"Something wrong."

"No, you have done nothing wrong.You need to work on some exercises. But from now on, not with me."

I didn't understand. "What do you mean?"

"You must have the consent of your parents."

"Parents consent?" I looked crooked at my coach. "What's going on, sir?"

He tenderly patted me on the head. "You were called to the Women's Gymnastics National Team of Romania. You were selected for Deva."

I was dumbstruck. I had heard of Deva. They were the best gymnasts in the country. Me? Deva? I felt again that I could cling to that star from my dream.

* * *

I expected that my parents would refuse the opportunity offered to me. It was very far from Bucharest. It would mean that we wouldn't see eachother often. But my parents were flexible, knowing what gymnastics meant to me. My coach had an important role in their decision. He spoke to them and I saw in my parents and my grandfather's eyes, sadness mixed with hope. I remained their only child and I knew that they would have liked to have me constantly beside them.

"How about you, Laura?" My father asked as serious he could be. "Would it be hard for you to stay away from us?"

"I don't know," I said sincerely. "But I love gymnastics and if I have talent and I'm good at it…" everything is good …

My answer was simple and quick. My mother smiled. So did my grandfather. Then I saw a twinkle in their dark eyes and my heart melted with hope and unexpected joy.

* * *

I packed my luggage for Deva with an inner peace and serenity that I hadn't felt for a long time. My dad took me and we traveled 8 hours by train. Mom drove us to the station quite relaxed about the idea of me being away. I don't know what she felt deep down in her soul, but her face displayed only peace in the moment when we said goodbye to each other. A broad smile lightened her face. Maybe she actually was happy for me and for my achievements.Maynbe she clung to them to soften the past, as a last hope.

It was a cold January and large flakes were dancing in the frosty air like white butterflies. It was cold, but I was warm from the emotions. I knew that the road I was to travel was the one I had chosen. It was my lucky star and the dream I was following fiercely.

I remembered in the train station the day when I first entered the gym. I already wanted to be among the winners. Nadia Comaneci was a winner. The first time I had seen her in competition, Micky and Is tarted to imitate her by lifting up our arms and legs as if we were ballerina dolls.

Then, few years later, she would come to workout right in our gym. I recognized her immediatly. "Oh, my God, Nadia herself," I chuckled. Nadia was on the beam and hid under it barely breathing. After she finished, I quickly ran off like a bird chased by a hunter. For me, Nadia Comaneci shone like a true diamond.

* * *

It continued to snow.

We had arrived earlier at the station, so I had time to say goodbye to my parents. I felt their deep love for me.

After some time, the train arrived. My mother promised to come see me at least twice a month. "Who knows, maybe more often" she said. "You are my soul, Laura. If you are not here, we're just surviving, not living."

I couldn't understand exactly what she meant. Only much later, years later, I would understand. When I had become a mother too.

"Come on, go and make me proud, my daughter. God be with you!" Then she whispered close to my ear: "You know, Micky is happy for you, in Heaven, right?"

I paused a moment, then I pursed my lips and I smiled, "I know, Mom. She's waving at me right now. She is nimble and lively."

My mother looked at me puzzled. "How do you know that? Are you sure?"

"Yes, Mother, I know. Just like you know that she is happy in heaven. Sun dances inside her mother."

"Sun also dances in you, Laura."

I kissed my mother and she kissed me back on both cheeks She waved until she faded to a shadow in the distance. I felt a pang, but I shook it quickly as I thought that I would see my mother soon. But I couldn't say the same thing about my grandfather. I still remember him weeping as he put 1000 lei in my right palm. "For a cake, my sweetie." I kissed his hand and I hugged him. My affection for my grandpa and his deep wrinkles on the cheeks will never fade. I knew he shared my happiness.

"When I see you on TV, my daughter, I will weep like a child."

"Perhaps you'll come along to Deva."

"Maybe. I don't know. Only Lord knows. I'm old, Laura."

"Yes, but you're healthy."

"Go, go with God, my girl. Let Heaven enlighten you!"

I looked lovingly at him and then I walked out the door, saying nothing more.

It had stopped snowing but the wind blew powerfully. It was hot in the train. I took off my gray coat revealing an orange sweater that my mother had bought. I talked to my dad but he slept after a while. I was traveling to find my way on the fragile way of life.

*   *   *

I had gymnastics in my blood. And I loved Cosmin more and more. It was a platonic childish love. When I announced to him that I was planning to go to Deva, he screamed in the street like a crazy person: "Victory!"

I asked his opinion, "Do you think it's a good thing, Cosmin?"

"What do you think girl?"

"I think I'm hanging by a star."

"Then hold on tight to it."

I started to laugh out loud, noisy and happy. It was the cheerful chatter of a two teenagers in love. He would have to go to Resita, he was selected in the men's gymnastic group. "What shall I do without you?" He said.

"You'll live," I laughed. "What do you think? Will your world collapse without me? No, I don't think so. You will be surrounded by many admirers and maybe I'll be forgotten. I hope that you won't, but who knows? But you will always remain in my soul."

"Oh, Laura, sometimes you say the strangest things. I'm sure there will come a day when you and I will look at the sun in the same place of the Universe."

*   *   *

The training program in Deva was very intense, but I forced myself to cope with it with stoicism. The sun shone through the ashy clouds over the city and it sen trays to warm my soul.

We woke up at 7:00 in the morning, we ate a very poor breakfast and then until 11:00, we had training. From 11:00 until 2:00-3:00, we went to school. We then relaxed beforewe finished the day with another workout. I knew that only through hard work I could reach the podium.

The girls were kind to me, including Ecaterina Szabo, Lavinia Agache (now they live in America). "The coach, Mr N.G., seemed like a lion trapped in a cage. Everything I did was wrong to him and he had me repeat every exercise until exhaustion. After several months, I was tired physically and mentally and my palms were bruised. I also lost weight due to lack of food. Bread was a rare product; we ate meat for protein and no sweets at all. Sweets, cakes, candies were banned completely.

Two weeks after moving to Deva, my father came loaded with a big bag full of food. When he saw me, his face was distorted. When we were alone in the room he said, "What's going on Laura? You are very thin."

I tried to smile, drained of my strength. "Sacrifice for fame, Dad!"

"Do you eat anything?"

"It's hard Dad, but please do not think that I'm complaining. Coach N.G. has something personal with Dinamo club, so he has something against me."

Dad's face was red with tension. "We have to do something. We must!"

I stopped him, "we can't do anything father. I will go forward and you and mom will come to visit me, as if nothing has happened."

"Do you think is better this way?"

"Yes, I have to follow my star."

"Listen young lady, I don't want to lose my baby because you have the goal of reaching some stupid star. If your mother sees you like this, what do you think she will say?"

"She will understand," I said resigned, with my head down.

"Yeah, right" he answered totally puzzled. He handed me the bag of food. "Here, eat something to get some strentgh."

I smiled bitterly. "We are not allowed, Dad. They weigh us every day. But... did you bringsome sweets?"

"Yes", he giggled. Then he asked, "why don't they allow this?"

"I don't know. They say we have to be slim, so they give us less food Daddy. That's why I've lost some kilos. But these sweets you brought me,

I will not give them up no matter what. I will share them with the other girls. I hope they will keep their mouth shut!"

"Ok my girl, but I told Coach N.G. to take good care of you. Why Laura, is so much evil on earth?"

"I think some people want to be bad and that's it."

My dad embraced me. He spent an hour with me and immediately after, I had to prepare for another workout. He left burdened with thoughts. I didn't want to upset him, but he saw the reality and we couldn't change it.

* * *

IT was March now. Even if the days were longer by several minutes, nature had yet to awaken to life yet. It was cold and the snow hadn't melted

I continued my training in the Great Hall, where I spent most of my time. Coach N.G. was always angry, but he was not angry with everyone. He had something against me. Always with me. Was it possible that my mind played some twisted trick on me and it was just my impression?

One day I was practicing an exercise on the beam and I fell twice. No, it wasn't from the hunger that tried my stomach but was from a lack of concentration. Hunger had become normal those days and some of the girls complained a lot. When my father had last come, he had brought a jar of instant coffee. We would scoop one spoonful of coffee with two teaspoons of sugar in a cup and eat it without water. That gave us energy and the girls thanked me for it.

After I had fallen the second time, N.G. who was watching me carefully, rushed towards me and without saying a word, he took me down like a doll. He grabbed my hair and he slammed my head against the beam. I felt severe pain and my hand went instinctively to my temples. My left brow was bleeding profusely. I looked at him defiantly though I kept my tears.

"Do you think that is right what you just did?"

"Go fix yourself," he said as if nothing serious had happened.

Everything was back to normal the very next day.

That night I dreamtof Micky again. I was telling her of my sufferings. We were somewhere in a green meadow where wonderful flowers arose here and there. We were smiling and wearing identical, pink dresses. At one point, I suddenly saddened. She took me gently by the hand."Hey, Laura, is your day becoming night?"

She was speaking like an adult. I started to cry and I told her about N.G. About the beating he had given me. She took her little finger and she put it softly to my broken brow, she comforted me and the pain disappeared mysteriously.

The next morning I felt the same serenity as in my dream. My sister was watching me beyond the grave.

"Micky, I whispered, I know you give me this peace. Thank you for praying to God for me, Micky."

I went to training like nothing happened and I entered again into that dizzying pace, as always. But the feeling of peace didn't leave my soul. I knew that Micky was my guardian angel.

*   *   *

Gymnastics world championships were approaching quickly, and we needed to have new routines, if not perfect, at least we had to strive for perfection.

N.G. seemed like a hysterical spinning top who couldn't cease. I didn't care about the hard work, but the hunger we all suffered, it started to affect me from all sides. I was very thin and I didn't grow very tall either.

The desire to conquer the podium was not suffering to me. The "Goddess of Montreal" was always on my mind. She suffered too, but then she tasted glory and everything had been brought as ahomage. During Ceausescu's era, athletes were not compensated financially. The only compensation was the steps made on the red carpet, and then walking proudly to the highest step on the podium. This ritual to glory, it makes you no longer want anything else. The applauses of the public fill your soul to the brim, and that state of "goodness" can't be explained in words.

One day I called home, full of enthusiasm and ready to face the world. My grandfather answered.

"Grandpa!"

He had a hoarse voice because of the bronchitis and although he hated pills, he had to take antibiotics.

"How are you, Grandpa?" I shouted into the receiver.

I felt he had tears in his eyes. I hadn't seen him for at least 3 months.

"Oh, my sweetie," grandfather mumbled hoarsely, "you can't imagine how happy I am to hear from you." He avoided telling me how much he missed me. He didn't want to affect me emotionally.

"I'll see you soon, Grandpa."

I felt the emotion in his voice. Tears flowed as he spoke. "How so, my girl?"

"I'm going to New York, Grandpa, to The America's Cup. I'm competing for Romania. Right now I'm really proud to be Romanian."

Emotions of joy and happiness burst like fireworks in my whole being. I had good news and I wanted to share it with all my dearest.

"Is mommy home?"

"Unfortunately not. She's at the grocery store but I will tell her. I am very happy for you. You know, Laura, I live only for you and I feel emotions through you."

"Thank you my good old grandpa. The sun is shining and the clouds have dissappeared."

The old man mumbled something else. I felt like I was there beside his green, velvet covered chair. When she came back home my mom called me. She also began to weep for joy.

"America, the promise land. You, my daughter, you have gotten me out of the darkness. I thought the sorrow had slipped into my life like an invisible thief who wanted to steal my soul."

Then I talked to my dad, who asked me when I would leave Deva and when he could come to the train station.

"Maybe your coach will let you visit us for couple of minutes."

"I hope so, Dad."

* * *

I went to America full of hope, curiosity and desire. N.G. allowed me to visit my folks. We had only half an hour at our disposal, but I made my family happy. My grandfather gave me a wooden cross with a crucified Jesus Christ. I humbly kissed the cross and hid it deep in one of my training suit pockets.

"Thanks, Grandpa. I'm sure it will help me."

My dad went with me to the airport and N.G appeared very benevolent in front of my father, but he had probably disguised his feelings. One day, when at Deva, my father saw me again with red, swollen eyes and he couldn't stand it. He went straight to N.G. and he told him in an authoritative tone, "Listen idiot! I didn't bring my child here to be tormented like this. I have only one child, not hundreds. Just think of how you would like to see your child struggling hard and slim as a greyhound. I'll take her out of here and Deva can go to hell. She can do something else with her life."

Then my father refused the coffee latte that N.G. prepared for him. Papa left angry and he wanted to take me back home. Only my love for gym persuaded him to leave me there. I never told my father that N.G. had hit myhead on the beam and had broken my brow bone. I said nothing because I knew for sure that if he found out, it would have been the end of my career. He would have taken me home and he would have started a huge scandal which would be heard at the Federation.

After that, N.G. changed his behavior.

New York was 8 hours away by plane, but we weren't bored. We talked about everything but gymnastics. We watched a comedy on one of televisions that hung above our heads.

We laughed with all our hearts and even N.G. dared to smile. I watched him. I was going to forgive him for what he had done to me and to my girls. I saw America at just 16 years old and I thank God for this. In a communist country, Ceausescu wouldn't let you pass anywhere. Even your door gate was controlled.

*   *   *

When we arrived early in the morning, I saw New York enveloped in such a dense fog that you could cut it with a knife. Through the smoky whiteness, I could see the city's lights. There were so many lights. At that time, in Romania, day or night, it was darkness no matter what. Here, in New York, everything was different. America deserved to be called the "Promised Land."

I likened New York to a modern fortress. It was amazing, but I felt a coldness that I had never felt at home.

Our accomodations were in a modern hotel. Something I had never seen in my life. I had been in other countries and in other luxury hotels but this was really something. It had surpassed them all. I was standing in front of the window, on the 30th floor and I looked down to the world, mesmerized by everything I saw. "So this is America." Like Christopher Columbus I intended to discover it, and then to conquer it.

*   *   *

The gym was very large. There was an enormous crowd who would applaud wildly for its favorite gymnasts. I was only 16 and a half years old and I felt like I was trying to see with my pinky finger. I was happy and a little nervous.

The stars began to shine now, like small, incandescent lights.

Then I heard Micky, somewhereabove, in her high heaven, like a gust of wind whispering: "Victory, Laura!" I felt that I was already victorious. I knew that the life of a gymnast was very short, it would be mixed with agony and ecstasy. I hoped more for ecstasy.

At the "America's Cup" in New York I came in 2nd place. I was on the podium like I had wished. I would have wanted more, I was thirsty for more. N.G. finally was satisfied and congratulated me for my performance.

That year Mary Lou Retton, the first gymnast of America, came first and she won all the glory.

I gave everything I had in me. I struggled to conquer the gold but in the end I stepped on the podium with an innocent smile and I show up in front of the whole world as if I would have to apologize for my failure, even there was no failure. My parents and my grandfather saw me in sports news and in the newspaper.

I called home and I talked to each one. Mother wept with joy, and my father and grandfather congratulated me. At one point, mom stopped crying and she said:

"I think Micky was with you, Laura."

"Yes, mom, she was with me. And I heard again that whisper blown by the wind."

My mother would never forget the child she got lost in that terrible accident. It was too much to ask her to forget Micky. She was always in my heart and my thoughts. The nights, for instance, when I couldn't sleep, I imagined her talking to me and encouraging me and sometimes I ask her to lend me some of her sweet serenity.

During the awards, people stood up and listened to America's national anthem. Their right hands over their hearts. I don't know why tears were coming down my cheeks. I had the vague feeling that in that moment even American people loved me.

The next day, we all flew back home. I was wearing a silver medal around my neck. I had wanted the gold, but even so, I began to feel proud of myself.

The giant plane flew through the clouds, and I passed also through them. The huge clouds looked like white or gray cotton. Then the sky became darker and it turned to night, and I, with the medal around my neck, climbed again on the most towering star.

* * *

At the World Championships in Budapest, Hungary, I had a new, never performed floor routine. I had to do it for the first time in a stadium packed with people, that would watch every move I made, as if I was a little bug under a microscope. I was aware that I could do something wrong and fall into disgrace. The pressure was incredible.

Octavian Belu, a referrence name in Romanian gymnastics and one of the greatest coaches in the world, encouraged me. Helping me to shake off all those strong emotions that I had.

"It's not a big deal, Laura," he said. "Just make a distraction of everybody. Imagine you're in rehearsal and you are just doing some ordinary routines."

And so I did. I just fell into positive thoughts and I did it. I got a good score and a humble smile lit up my face. I succeeded once again.

* * *

America's Cup was the same year as the Los Angeles, California Olympics. I was so happy to be back in the "promised land."

For this important competition, we would fly on a special plane for the Romanian athletes, reporters and photographers who will participate in America's Cup. It was pretty overwhelming, and our trainingwas doubled, but none of us felt like victims. N.G. and Octavian Belu gave us a new challenge and all the girls accepted it.

"Hey girls, what do you say we win Gold this year?"

We wanted this too. We already dreamed of touching and caressing the golden medals with the 5 Olympic circles. What could an athlete want more than that?

One evening, after all the girls in the room were asleep, I went to the bathroom to pray. I fell on my knees and I gathered in my hands the cross that grandfather gave to me. Then I said a prayer to Jesus and to Saint Virgin Mary. I asked them to protect us all and to give us peace and happiness. I didn't have the courage to ask more. I felt that night, a need to pray that I couldn't remember having before. I went to God with all my heart and I embraced him with all my being. Then after the prayer, I felt an indefinite gratification that only divinity can bestow.

* * *

First we saw the Pacific coast, then the breathtaking, panoramic view of L.A. It was fascinating, this second largest city in the U.S., right after New York. It was also known as the most expensive city in the world and perhaps the richest.

Our plane arrived from accross the world. All of the passengers including myself applauded the captain and his crew for our safe arrival.

"It's wonderful!" I chuckled to Lavinia Agache who tapped me lightly on the shoulder.

"Here we will make it work, or we will have to hide in the bushes like some imposters," she said.

I raised my eyebrows, wondering what she meant But Lavinia smiled calmly and dignified like a princess.

We arrived in Los Angeles, California on a hot, Wednesday afternoonat 4:10. At the airport, we were greeted by hundreds of people with flowers.

We were tired after 17 hours of flying but we forgot almost immediately our weariness and were all smiles for the photographers who hoped to catch a picture of us. We were nervous, but this time, the emotions were constructive. I again heard the sweet whisper of my sister, "Victory Laura."

*   *   *

The Romanian Delegationand the other participating countries, were welcomed at the Opening Ceremony by more than 100,000 people from all over the world. I walked in front of the crowd proud of my country (in those days I forgot that I lived in communism). All of the athletes had the same uniform: a skirt, blouse, jacket and an elegant hat. The men wore the same color of pants and shirts.

I admired these people, Romanian or foreign who devoted their lives to their sport.

The Ceremony was magnificent. I had never seen so much color or so much beauty. Yes, Lavinia was right, we needed to give our best herefor glory. Here, where all the elite of our sport were gathered.

Nadia Comaneci was also with us, encouraging us as much as she could. She had retired from competition on May 6 of that year.We had visited Disneyland together and we had our group pictures taken with Donald and the Mouse family.

During the games, we were lived at UCLA, a prestigious Californian university. We drove about 40 minutes in yellow school buses to Pauley Pavilion, where the gymnastics competitions would take place. The buses were overflowing with journalists and photographers, a sign that gymnastics would always be in the media spotlight. This is what my life was made of and I found myself among those stars, the stars of gymnastics world.

The Olympics were televised in Romania, so I was sure my parents and my grandfather were watching. My mother told me once that when I competed on uneven bars, her courage left her instantly and she covered her eyes with her hand. It was too much for her. Too many emotions. Then when she saw that I scored well, she wept for joy, a joy that lightened her soul. I needed to know that she was happy. If she was smiling again, then I was overcome with hapiness.

I competed at this Olympics with a sprained leg. I felloff the beam and I saddened the entire world. But as a team, we conquered the Gold. The Romanian team were winners in L.A.

When all six girls stepped on the podium, we were intensely watched by cheering fans and athletes. The room was huge, larger than the one we were in at The America's Cup. At that time, Romania had different hymn, "Three Colors," but now we have another one, "Wake Up, Romanian." The latter is more humane, full of hidden power and meaning that only we, as Romanians could understand. But back in that time, even if "Three Colors" played for us, we were all proud to be there, on the podium.

The Romanian team had become Olympic champions. What's more to tell about it? Everything was forgotten. The hunger, the training, the home sickness.

I recieved dozens of letter from fans. The letters were in English and Spanish. I knew some English, but I had no idea what my Spanish fans were saying. I also received pictures of my fans. One of them was of a handsome Argentine who flashed the most beautiful smile as he climbed a mountain covered in snow. "A thousand kisses" he wrote in Spanish (a Spanish friend of mine translated it into English). The picture came bundled with a rather long letter in which he asked me to marry him. God, I was just a kid! I started to laugh when she told me in broken English what the Argentinian wanted.

Over time, I received many marriage proposals from all over the world, even from men 30 years old or older! My heart and soul overflowed with joy at that time.God had really blessed me!

I went shopping in L.A. with the girls. I bought a dress for my mother. It was dark blue with white dots. My mother still mourned. I also purchased a sweater for grandpa and a polo shirt for dad. I was very pleased with all my purchases.I couldn't wait to get home and give them to my dearests.

I missed them a lot. I missed Cosmin too. I hadn't heard from him for awhile. He gave everything to the sport like I did. For about 6 years, Cosmin was part of National Team. He competed in many national and international competitions.

I missed him, but I was also upset with him. He didn't give any signs. He discarded me from his life like I was an useless rag. However, in the depths of my soul, I made excuses for him. Maybe he couldn't, maybe it was too hard for him, he mightnot know how to contact me... Then one day I stopped wondering. Wasn't it him who promised me that one day we would see the sunrise together? The only thing I had left was to believe.

He was still in my heart and my soul, though, handsome boys swarmed around me. They were gentle and they smiled at me. They kindly kissed my hand but I never crossed the line. They asked me for the phone number, but I always politely declined or I was very ambiguous.

I didn't consider myself a celebrity. Even as we arrived back in Romania, hundreds of people were waiting for us at the airport. My parents, my grandfather and a few close relatives. The Romanian Delegation came home that year with 53 medals, 20 of which were gold. This placed our country in second place of all nations.

I think Dictator Ceausescu was full of joy and contentment that his socialist and communist country Romania excelled in front of the world.

I received dozens of roses and I gave interviews. But all I wanted was to hug my sweet mother. I cut through the crowd, as I saw her waving her hand. Soon, I fell into her arms and I lovingly embraced her. She was weeping and she kissed me on the forehead.

"Why are you crying, Mommy?" I asked her and I wiped her tears.

"I'm happy!" she sighed.

"I thought so," I smiled.

Then I became serious. "You know, Mom, Micky was there with me."

She embracedmein her arms and her tears bathed against her cheeks.

"I knew it! I knew it!" she whispered.

I hugged my father and my grandfather too.

"Grandpa's girl!" He said and the old man stretched out his arms. "You're a miracle to me, you are the sunshine of my life."

I kissed him on both cheeks. I was a miracle for him only because I was breathing. My relatives all waiting to be embraced. In those moments I was really happy.

*   *   *

I stayed home almost two weeks. I cut my hair. I had long hair at the Olympics and I used to pull it back in a ponytail. One day, I walked with my cousins all over Bucharest and we watched all kinds of movies. People recognized me on the street, even with shorter hair. I was happy. I thanked God for this priceless gift he had given me - my talent.

I met again with my coach, Mr. Stefanescu, the first man who guided my steps to victory.

"I was very proud of you, Laura. I cheered for you with all my heart."

I laughed cheerfully and I looked up at him. "I say that you are the best coach in the world."

My father hosted a dinner in my honor and all my relatives were invited. I gave them American cigarettes and Jack Daniels whiskey, which in those days were rare, luxurious things.

"These things can only be purchased here if you have connections," said my uncle, enjoying the cigarette and tasting the drink. "In this country, you can't find anything in the market. How is America, Laura?"

I responded promptly. "Just as they say. The Promised Land."

During that time, I spoke with many people. Some people felt sorry for my failure on the beam and they tried to comfort me. "There will be other competitions, Laura."

But there wouldn't be another Olympics for me.

However, the team had become Olympic champions and that was something that many people wouldn't even dare to dream about.

Those were the best days of my youth. My mother made the best dishes, and my father brought me cakes. I ate all the goodies without thinking of the weight that I would gain. I actually didn't gain one kilo. I slept until late, took a cold shower when I woke up and ate everything that crossed my path.

That winter, two men from the U.S. Embassy visited my home. They wanted to know more about me and get to know me personally. My grandfather spoke to them in very good English. He had lived years ago in America when he was very young. He tried to teach me some English, but unfortunately it didn't appeal to me too much. Sport were my number one priority.

"You see, Laura, you didn't want to make an effort to learn English. If you would have, you could talk to these gentlemen," grandfather said.

"I know, Grandpa, it's too late now for apologies. I will learn, I promise."

The Americans stayed with us until morning. They drank Jack Daniels and smoked fine Cuban Cigars. We took lots of pictures with them. I modeled my official uniform. Romanian jacket and the hat. They were happy, I was happy. Mom made the best Romanian cuisine and we felt great. It was a Merry Christmas with a huge fresh Christmass tree and a lot of silver tinsel.

* * *

After the Olympics, I was trained by the legendary Nadia Comaneci. Despite her amazing talent, the young coach was modest and charming. I was glad for these moments.

* * *

I went to a competition in Germany under the magic wand of Nadia Comaneci. Some new girls were chosen for the team, including Madalina Tanase. I immediatley took to her. I considered her my sister.

"Are you afraid of something Laura?" She asked me one day.

I answered: "Yes, I'm afraid of not seeing Cosmin ever again."

She giggled and she took my hand. It was night, and the stars flickered like fireflies. "Do you see the stars?" She pointed her finger to the sky.

"You told me that your sister is among them. Well, I think she will lead you to the one you love."

"Yes, but it's been a long while since he called" I replied, upset.

"He has his reasons, don't you think?"

And Madalina was right. One day, my little star, I mean Micky, brought Cosmin and I together. Physically and spiritually. When I saw him at a hotel where we were staying in Germany. My eyes filled with tears. He was taller than I remembered him and very handsome. "A true Adonis," I said to myself.

His gaze found me, he smiled with all his heart. I felt like I was melting. He hugged me tightly and then he kissed me on the forehead.

"The shadows of past always haunted me," he said.

I was touched.

"Why didn't you give me any sign of life?"

He just said: "It was meant to be. But now we are here, alone, in a cold foreign country."

"We loved each other, didn't we?" I dared to ask. "We were two teenagers in love, weren't we?"

He kissed me again on the forehead. "What do you think?"

"I don't know," I said.

"There will come a time when we'll know."

He took me in his arms and he lifted me up. He had such strong muscles.

"You shone in L.A. Like a real star."

"Let's not exaggerate," I said.

"I had sweaty palms every time you competed. I thought my heart would pop out of my chest. Like I said, shadows of the past always haunted me, though."

"Are the girls swarming around you?"

"I don't know."

"You don't want to tell me?" I asked jealously.

He began to laugh, showing his white teeth. I wondered how many times a day he brushed his teeth? I gave him a gentle nudge in the stomach.

"Answer me, should I have reasons to be jealous?"

"I don't know. You know better. But one day, we'll look at the sky and we will be together forever."

"You're lying!"

"I don't lie."

Suddenly he became serious. I kissed him on the cheek and left him to watch me enter the hotel elevator. Cosmin was back in my life and he promised he would never leave again. At least, that is what I thought in that moment.

*   *   *

After the nights training, I took a shower then I wrapped myself in my bath robe made of a real towel that I took with me everywhere. It was comfortable and I felt that I had a little piece of home with me.

"Madalina, I saw Cosmin."

"Yes, me too. He is a really cool guy."

We started to giggle.

I was a teenage girl dreaming about love. Like Romeo and Juliet.

*   *   *

One night I woke up from a dream.

It was very cold outside. I felt like I was flanked by a freezing wind. I knew it was a dream, but I still felt cold throughout my entire body. I sat up and looked around. Madalina slept, uncovered like a log in the other bed and I realized that the room was actually quite warm. I didn't know where the terrible cold had come from. I thought it would have been nice to have Cosmin near me. He could give me a hot kiss if he wanted, it could be enough.

I got up from bed and I suddenly felt the urge to take a hot shower. I moved around slowly, because I didn't want to wake up my friend. I got out of bed carefully and made hot lime tea with sugar. I drank it sip by sip. I wanted it to melt from my body the intense cold that had penetrated my bones.

I looked out of the window. It had started to snow. During the preceding day, the sun hadn't shown at all. A few threatening clouds were foretelling a miserable time.

The chill wasgone. I put the empty cup on the nightstand then I pulled the duvet over me. Slowly, I felt the warmth embracing me and a humble smile appeared on my lips. It was fine now.

*   *   *

The next day the snow had stopped, but the wind blew. We dressed then went to breakfast. At the table, Cosmin Licaciu looked stuck up. I felt he was upset. Why didn't he flash me one of his charming smiles? As we left, he caught my arm.

"Hey, not even a hello?"

I pulled my arm from his hand.

"Are you upset, Sir?" I wanted to seem cool, but I felt a kind affection flowing inside of me. He tried to smile but he managed only a pathetic grimace.

"Yes, Laura, you're right, I'm upset. I hurt my ankle and I don't know if I can compete.

I sympathized with his pain and I felt sorry for him. I knew the feeling very well, so I hugged him with all my pure, teenage love.

"I'm sorry".

He took my hand and he led me down the aisle, to a secluded place.

"I'm sorry too, but a part of me is glad because I think we are soul mates, right?"

Instead of an answer, I kissed him lightly on the cheek.

"It will be fine. The sun never sets for us, remember? If it sets here, it will rise elsewhere. And so on."

Cosmin tried to smile, but he winced in pain again.

"Let me help you. Lean on me," I said worried.

I helped him up to his room. In the lobby, our team mates smiled. They nicknamed us "love birds." Even our coach, Mr. Octavian Belu knew about our love. One day he told me:

"You will be called Laura Licaciu. L.L. as B.B. You'll be famous."

I laughed at him loudly. I felt I was the envy of the other girls.

In the evening, when we all gathered together in the hallway, the other girls followed Cosmin with their eyes, throwing him glances and sweeter than honey smiles. They looked at me like I was an intruder.

After the competition, Cosmin, who competed with a swollen ankle, went to Resita, and I went back to Deva. When we separated, he hugged me in his strong arms, he kissed me on the forehead, as he used to. He whispered in my ear: "One day, you and I will watch the sunset in the same place. Soon."

* * *

1986 was bad for my career as a gymnast. I had a broken elbow, my back was injured enough to miss competitions. To top it off, I bit my knee while doing some jumps. The knee became infected and I could see to the bone. I couldn't practice, so I stayed home per the doctors instructions. I took many antibiotics and I walked for long time on one leg, hanging on dad who helped me walk where I needed.

That year I didn't participate in any competitions. I had the impression that my life was changing. It seemed that my whole world had collapsed.

I moved back to Bucharest.

On August 23, 1944, Romania was liberated from the fascist yoke. I wasn't a history lover, but my Grandpa insisted that I know why Romanians put such an emphasis on this day. Everyone brought odes to Ceausescu. I really didn't understand and honestly, I didn't care.

In Bucharest I was in love. Cosmin went to the same club I did.He had been at the club Dinamo few years ago.

In those sunny yet sad days (the period after the death of Micky), Madalina Tanase became my best friend.

I spent most of my time at the Club "23 August. Mom and Dad came to see me, but there were days when I would sit at home in my old child hood room. "Is it all over here?" I wondered. "My gymnastics career ends here, like a tree cut from its roots?"

I felt like I was missing something. A piece of me that couldn't be recovered again. A huge piece suddenly lost after 10 years of uninterrupted gymnastics.

Then one day at training, I broke my hand.The doctors couldn'tset it correctly. It was like they wanted to get rid of me. I stayed in the hospital for two weeks. Cosmin Licaciu came every day to see me, as if he was waiting for a miraculous healing.

Now I could eat freely, whatever I desired. Somehow, I knew my gymnast career is was nearing its end. Too physcal and mental injuries. Sometimes I felt lost. What was to happen to my future? I couldn't see it shining again.

One day, while I was sitting on the bench with my arm tied around my neck, Cosmin came to see me. It was hot outside. Wind carried the leaves away. It was sunny, autumn morning and the light danced on my face.

How is my little patient?" he asked me and kissed me lightly on the lips.

It was the first time he had done that and I felt a thousand butterflies dancing in my stomach. I loved him. I didn't think I could be in love with someone so much. His lips were soft and moist and I said: "I want more."

He gave me a cheerful, inquisitive look.

"More cookies? Here they are" and he handed me a boxfull of cookies.

They were called "La Boheme" and they were very rich and creamy. They were my favorite cookies but I preferred his sweet kiss.

"More," I bravely repeated.

He understood what I meant but he teased me for a few a while. Eventually he kissed me again, more passionately than the first time.

My boyfriend who was in love with me. My head was spinning and I didn't think I could keep my feet on the ground.

"Why are you doing this?" I asked him.

"Don't you think it's time?"

"Don't you see that I'm melting?"

I expressed my feelings to him knowing he would never betray me. Sunlight danced on his beautiful face, bathing it in a calm light.

He took my healthy hand and he led me to the lounge. He helped me sit on the hospital bed and he put a pillow under my head. Then he sat next to me. It seemed he hadn't heard my last question, but he did. He kissed me again and I felt like I was floating somewhere between Heaven and Earth. He whispered, "I'm melting too."

He gently caressed my face with his fingers, as if he wanted me to remember my features.

"What do you know? You know nothing."

"Really?"

"For instance, do you know that we're soul mates? Neither of us could live without the other one you know?"

"Are you sure?" I laughed.

He remarked, "You have such a beautiful white teeth."

"What?" I mumbled.

"Kiss me more." He said.

"You have given me hope to go on. You know how to push my buttons."

"Are you happy now, Laura?"

"In this moment, yes, I'm happy." I was sure of it.

He took my hand. "Listen, Laura, I want to tell you something."

He moistened his lips with his tongue and continued:

"A spirit comes before God and told him: "God, why when we were good, were only two sets of footprints in the sand, and when everything goes wrong, it was just one? Where were you when I needed you?"

And Lord answered," When everything was right, I was next to you, so that's why there were two sets of footprints. When you saw only one set of footprints and you thought that things were going bad, you were actually being carried away in my arms. Therefore, there was only one set of footprints. Mine."

"Now do you understand, Laura?"

I did understand and I also had goosebumps.

"God protects us all, we are his children."

My friend's parable enlightened my soul. "You are a wise guy, you know that?"

"Yes, I know," he laughed. "And you are a small goldfish swimming in muddy water. This period I mean. But water will clear soon, you will see. You are incredibly young and beautiful and life is smiling at you from all its corners, but you don't realize it yet."

I felt relieved. His words were like a bandage to my wounded soul.

"I know you want to be coach. You will be! Turn yourself over to God and don't worry."

I hadn't had the opportunity to meet his spiritual side, but I was glad I had found it and that both believed the same. We were on the same wavelength and, as he said, we were soul mates.

I was daydreaming how I wanted him in my life as a talisman of good fortune. I was proud to be his girlfriend. He is a man who knew how to filter the light and share it with everyone. Especially with me.

*   *   *

One day I asked him Cosmin:

"Why are you doing this for me? Dozens of beautiful girls would feel lucky to be with you."

The sun fell lightly over the city. He looked calmly to the sunset. He stayed silent for awhile. One moment, two, three … it seemed an eternity to me.

"Cosmin?"

He kept silent until a pleasant smile lit up his face.

"Yes? Did you say something?"

"Yes."

I thought maybe he didn't want to answer me, so I didn't pressure him. I wanted him to say, "I love you Laura, I'm fond of you and the sun never rises without you."

"You asked me why I'm doing this. It's like asking me why the sun rises and sets. It's the natural course of things, Laura."

I was silent. I don't know why I was jealous, I had all of him for me.

"Natural course of things." Did that mean he would go to any person who was suffering, giving of himself completely?

"Laura?"

His voice was so delicate that I felt like crying with emotion. I sat staring at the sunset, as he had done earlier. He kissed me on the neck and I felt shivers up my back.

"Are you playing with me?" He asked me through kisses.

"No, no, you're playing with me. I don't know why you are doing this to me, I don't know why you travel every day to see me.

I started to cry. All those feelings overwhelmed me. Had I fallen into some kind of depression? I didn't know why I was complaining so much and where this anger had been hidden for so long. Actually, the question was: what did I want? Cosmin hugged me.

"Come on, cry! You have been here too long and this place smells of rot and your thoughts have darkened. You're a strong girl, Laura and I am beside you. Simple. You needed a cry and that's all. Come on, cry, just let go" he said again, kissing my face while holding me tightly in his arms.

I wiped my tears. I tried to smile and I finally succeeded.

"That's it!" He said. "This is the most beautiful smile that I've ever seen."

We embraced tightly then, seeing that it was getting dark, I said:

"It's time for you to go home. Run, the sun is setting. I want you to get home safely."

"I want to see your face always happy, but I know that's impossible." He rose from the bed and put a finger to his lips and then touched my lips.

I nodded as I moistened my lips. As I watched him walked out the door, I thought I could never love a man more in this world. My love blossomed like flowers in the spring.I hoped the flowers of my love would never fade.

*   *   *

Madalina Tanase was moving in her bed in the dark room. We lived together in the same room. It was the end of a cold November and all my joints hurt, especially my broken hand and my entire back.

"Look at me! I sound like an old lady who has just turned 80," I said. What nonsense, because if I were to start over, I would still choose gym. Even without material satisfactions. We lived in a country where people have to shut their mouths in order to stay alive. Nobody has anything to say and if somebody made a mistake, he was thrown immediatly into jail."

Madalina sighed and continued to rub her hands and feet.

"Hey, what's with you?" I said.

"Come on, leave me alone, I'm nervous." She said.

"Why?"

"Because of this disgusting life and... I can't sleep."

I put my pillow under my back and lit the small silver metal lamp. "Come on, talk to me. I can't sleep either."

"What could I tell you? I feel nothing. I'm disgusted that we live in a country where there's no opportnities, no motivation, nothing."

"It is the country where we were born and that's the situation." I said.

She turned on her belly and she wrapped the pillow with her arms. "Well, tell me... how's Cosmin?

I didn't understand what she wanted to know. "How is Cosmin? Meaning?" Then I realized. "Oh, well... imagine ... like a stallion," I giggled.

"You're such a liar! You just want to play my game, right? I know you haven't slept with him. I know," and she laughed beating her fist on the pillow.

"Why are you asking then?"

"Just like that, I wanted to catch you lying."

"Well, I haven't slept with him and you know that. He hasn't even seen me naked."

Madalina chuckled. "Really?"

"Really", I nodded.

"You are kind of silly, you know?"

"Who cares?"

We continued to talk about many other trifles, for instance about the fact that some girls were drooling after my boyfriend and about the letters that I kept recieving.

"Do you know that there is an Indonesian man who wants to marry me?" I confessed to Madalina. "He's filthy rich."

"Then do whatever is necessary to get your hands on him!"

"In Jakarta there were princesses with crowns and all that stuff. I think that's where he saw me."

"You think so? And?"

"And what?"

"Don't you see the sunshine in your life, even if mist covers everything else?"

"Let's not exaggerate! I'm not going to have "Asian eyes kids." And my love for Cosmin is too great."

"Okay, okay. Let's go back to sleep."

"How will I do that? I feel like I have toothpicks in my eyes. I can't close my eyelids. Sometimes I feel that life plays with us, it doesn't make sense."

"Don't talk nonsense, you are young and the stars dance for you."

Madalina had turned off the lamp and the room was in thick darkness.

*   *   *

It was getting dark. It was a day with frost and the sun didn't show at all, as if wanting to rest in its favorite places. It was cold, but warmth reigned in the room.

Madalina had a date with a weightlifter. I laughed when she told me, I don't know why, weightlifters are people too. I imagined her small and fragile, hand in hand with this weightlifter, big and so blocky.

"Be carefull! I will be late," she said. "We are going to a coffee shop, then to a movie."

I nodded, "Go wherever you want, Mada. Just beware!"

I turned on the TV, but on the news, they paid another homage to Ceausescu. I turned it off and swore softly.

"If I want, I could leave this country," I thought to myself. "I can't figure out why I haven't. I would take Cosmin with me and we could fly right through the clouds to the "Promised Land.""

I thought quite a lot of escape but I also thought of my parents and grandparents. Soon, I will be done with gymnastics and I will be with them, watching over them like an angel. Since Mickey died, they clung to me and we were a united and loving family.

Somebody beat on the door and wok eme wake from my sweet daydream. I flinched slightly and asked who is was.

"The star that lights up your life," I heard Cosmin's voice.

I opened the door immediately and I said playfully:

"The star on which I gladly climbed."

"I heard you were alone," he said.

He looked amazing! He was wearing a blue tracksuit with red stripes. I have to admit, Cosmin always had exquisite taste in clothing, which made him even more attractive. My legs almost gave out. He was the man of my dreams. God, I loved him so much.

He entered and he closed the door behind him, then pulled the latch. He approached slowly as he didn't want to bother the scent of love floating in the air.

"I love you!" He told me, without any other introduction. "Don't you believe me, Laura?

"No! Of course!" I broke out laughing like crazy. "I believe you.

He didn't say anything (although I was expecting him to say something). My heart was pounding, almost beating through my chest.

His gaze burned my skin. I didn't know if it was a simple illusion, but his eyes sparkled. He took me in his arms and put me carefully on the bed. Emotions overwhelmed me.

"You smell so nice," he said.

Then we kissed, as we did before, and our tongues were merged, dancing their specific dance. He kissed my face, then slowly, he took every part of my body, tasting and admiring it. I wanted to make a move, but he stopped me. He continued to kiss my fingers, my hands and my feet in a slow, rhythm.We continuously kissed for over an hour.

After a while, he sat next to me and he took me in his arms and he said:

"You're just a bud blooming now."

I was confused. Why didn't he make love to me? He knew I would do it. Cosmin had a special kind of love for me that night, the one involving respect and fear, and I loved him even more for that.

*   *   *

There were many hot nights like this, when the sun was setting to the west, and the sky was icy. Madalina would go out with her boyfriend and Cosmin would sneak into our room. We loved each other and we were happy. However, after the iniverse fade, a chain of sad events overwhelmed me and they left deep scars on my heart. Eventually, after 11 years of dedication, I had to quit gymnastics. The feeling of emptiness overtook my heart.

Cosmin continued his gymnastics training. He did everything in his power to make me happy. My parents and my grandfather encouraged me too. "Let it be, Laura, let it be! You have worked so hard... legs and hands broken... a lifetime dedicated to your sport."

I was smiling and hugging him lovingly. My loving daddy who he had made dozens of trips to Deva to see all these years! I appreciated all three of them. I gave them joy, excitement and sadness, which caused them to go forward. Nobody forgot Micky. She still occupied a special place in my heart and my mind, from where she was always smiling warmly.

I felt her closer and I spoke to her in my dreams and when I was awake. I spoke to her every night when I went to bed and in the morning when I woke up. I know she hears me, I was firmly convinced of this.

Grandpa showed signs of fatigue and sometimes he was very sick. He had dizziness and head aches. The symptoms would come and go, scaring us all. He's old and I didn't expect him to live forever, but I couldn't bear the thought that he may leave us soon.

One afternoon, my grandfather dranksome tea in the courtyard under vines full of green grapes. He had lost so much weight. His skin hung in folds around his neck. I felt very sorry for him and I didn't want him to suffer.

"Do you want to sit on grandfather's lap, Laura?" He asked me with a shaky voice.

"Well, Grandpa," I mumbled, thinking I was too big for this and he wouldn't have the strength to hold me.

"Come on, Laura, sit on grandpa's lap," he repeated.

I sat down carefully on his leg, paying attention to not crush him under my weight and I kissed his wrinkled face and the bags under his bloodshot eyes. He smiled, but it was a faded smile, out of place. I called it later "the smile of death."

"Laura," he started, "you know that Grandpa loves you a lot. I loved your sister too and, you know, she always talks to me."

I wanted to say, "Do you also talk to her, Grandpa?" Everyone in the house seemed to do that, but we didn't admit it to one another.

"Yes, Grandpa, I know."

"Laura ..." Grandpa's voice suddenly became barely audible and I realized that it was drowning in tears. My grandfather was crying.

"Why are you crying, Grandpa?" I asked him worried.

"Because the sun is down, Laura." He lifted up his hand and waved it from side to side. "Not for you. For me, Laura. The sun is down for me. I'm falling also, but I'll be happy beside Micky."

I began to cry softly. "Grandpa, don't say that! Why is everyone I love leaving me?

Grandfather wiped his tears. "Listen to me, Laura. I was happy throughout your career. I watched your gymnastics and I stayed by your side saying prayers for you. You made an old man so unbelivably happy. I'm approaching 90 years old and I feel I need to travel elsewhere. Who knows, perhaps to a better world."

"Grandpa ..." now I was crying like a baby.

"Don't cry, please," he patted me on the head, "just spend with me my last days. Then, maybe we will communicate one day through our dreams or ..."

"Daydreaming ..." I said through tears.

"Yes, in your daydreaming ... when my voice will echo in your ears like tinkling bells you will know that is me. What do you think?"

"I don't want you to die, Grandpa, that's what I think," I said. "I want you to stay with me, my dear old man," I started to cryout loud, hugging him hard.

"Come on, Laura, please don't cry."

"How do you know that you gonna die?" I asked.

"I'm sick and very old, my dear."

* * *

My grandfather died a few days later. I was there next to him, like he wanted, I didn't have the power to feel joy for him as I knew he had wanted. Another piece of my soul had left.

Micky and grandpa were together now. And I am here on Earth, worn by loss.

* * *

It was a sunny summer day and the sun was working hard. I sat under a canopy of vines, sipping lattes. I simply listened to my thoughts.

All my thoughts and dreams converged to Cosmin Licaciu. I smiled and I sipped my little, hot drink even though outside was almost degrees. I was thinking of his beautiful body and his childish face. We had seen each other two days before. He seemed slightly irritated. I asked him what was wrong but he did nothing but kissing me passionately.

"I want to see you again, Laura. I'm hungry for you. I want you badly and one day you will be mine."

I thought to myself, "You can have me right now, silly you can feel me and love me." But I said nothing. We separated at Herastrau park, promising another rendezvous.

Now I waited for his phone call. We were supposed to meet tonight. I imagined his hands touching my breasts and a deep silence overwhelmed me. I sat in silence for a while, I don't know for how long, five or ten minutes, then I heard the sound of the phone breaking the silence of the night.

I flinched and I ran through the house, down the hall-way.

"Hello?"

I could hear the smile in his voice.

"I want to see you, baby! In Herastrau."

"Yes, I want to see you too," I chuckled.

I hung up the phone, after he sent me a kiss that I returned back to him over the phone. I took a shower and put on a short green dress. I left in hurry with wet hair, no makeup, saying good bye to my mother, who stood at the gate talking to a neighbor.

"Where are you running to like this, Laura?"

"To see Cosmin."

My mother knew about my friendship with Cosmin. She had met him at my 18th birthdayparty and she was delighted with him. My mother smiled at me and she continued to talk to her neighbor.

* * *

It was a pleasant autumn with rusted leaves that were falling onto the dry pavement. The clouds were white like giants bales of cotton. Not a drop of rain, only a soft breeze.

Meanwhile, my hair had dried and it became wavy. Thebreeze ravaged my curls.Daniel Cosmin was sitting on a bench in Herastrau, tearing one by one the petals off of a daisy and throwing them into a puddle.

"Why are you breaking these flowers?" I scolded him teasingly. "They are made to admire, not to break apart."

The young man stood up, as if on command. I immediately noticed that he was slightly disheveled and I felt something weird in my stomach, like a gloomy feeling. He kissed my lips.

"How are you, princess?" He asked as we sat on a wooden green bench. Two old ladies right across the street were chatting like two cheerful sparrows.

"Laura, we need to talk. Listen to me," he said and he kissed my hands.

My heart began to race like a horse. I was torn now because I didn't know what was coming. It seemed to be something serious and I loved him so much!

"I want to get married."

I started to cry. I wasn't prepared for such a offer. Nor for marriage.

"We're too young," I answered, "but yes, I want to marry you. Yes, yes, yes, eventually."

"Now, Laura," he said firmly.

"You must be joking," I said totally confused and annoyed.

"Why the rush?"

"Why do we have to hurry. It's a big decision!"

"No, I'm not kidding," he attempted a smile, but it came out a grimace. "I'm leaving, Laura, I'm leaving with the circus."

Cosmin had recently taken a job in Bucharest at the Circus.

"The army wants me," he continued. "The circus is my plan to get back to the Promised Land. And you ... I want you to come with me."

My eyes suddenly overflowed with tears. "My parents would be alone and I am not prepared for that."

"You promised me that we would see the sun together, married. Why don't you want to keep your word?"

"I'm doing my best to keep my word. We will see the sunrise but in another world, a better one."

"Maybe from your point of view. In fact, what do you understand by a better world? A world where the wolf and the lamb are good friends?"

I wiped a tear that was rolling down my cheek.

"That world doesn't exist. You are wrong."

He took my arm, and I saw on his face a mixture of confusion and sadness.

"I love you, Laura," he said as if this was his last effort.

"If you love me, don't go. Stay with me."

"I can't. You have to understand."

I shook my arm from his hand, I turned my back and I walked away. I didn't know if I was doing the right thing, but I left. He softly whispered my name, but he didn't move.

"Laura!" I heard my name again.

I continued to walk forward. I cried and the sadness filled my soul. I knew one thing for sure. I wouldn't see him again. For a long, long time.

*   *   *

I finished high school and I harbored some hope for the future. I wanted to work at the club Dinamo as a coach, to help other children fulfill their dreams. Dreams, that will inflate like balloons, then they will break from the reality.

I was 21 and I started to dream again. The letters were still filling my mail box. They kept coming. I could have chosen my husband from one of my fans, but I didn't. I also had my admirers in Bucharest. They sent me flowers that make me feel desired.

I always thought of Cosmin. I missed his touches and caresses, his soft lips. Sometimes I still felt them on my skin.

I had lost him forever. He was so far away in another part of the world. I tried to forget him and I did everything to do that. I threw away my old clothes and I shopped for new ones. I made myself busy so I didn't have time to think of him. Only in my dreams, when I would touch his beautiful face.

Meanwhile, my mother fell ill. She complained of strong abdominal pain.The color of her face and her features changed. I was worried. We had had enough pain in our family already. The suffering seemed to be have allied with us, making it a kind of family member. She started drinking more tea and eating more natural, but even so, the pain became unbearable. Sometimes the pain disfigured her, reaching unbearable thresholds. I decided to take her to the hospital emergency. She was barely able to walk, so we took a taxi. I had no car.

My mother stayed in the hospital for two weeks for investigation, and then we had to return for her operation. The doctors were still investigating, and we waited for the diagnosis.

It was the beginning of December. The sun, shone occasionally in the sky. At that time, Communist Europe was boiling, and communism was falling apart. I was happy knowing that we wouldget rid of Ceausescu.

"We will have food," people cried in the streets. They didn't care that they could be arrested. Their voices had been stiffled for decades. They smiled and cried for happiness, even if the revolution in December '89 was a political one.

My mother had the surgery right then, when emergency hospital was riddled with army's bullets and unseen enemies. My father and I sat in the lobby, drinking coffee with milk and trying to be courageous. After surgery, my mother had a colostomy bag.

"Why, Laura? What's with this bag?" She asked me very upset. "I want to be healthy again."

"But you are healthy now, mom. The doctors will fix the problem with the bag," I lied to her. In fact, I didn't know how long she would have the bag.

One day I asked the doctor, "Excuse me, when will you remove my mother's bag?"

"Come to my office," he said.

We entered a small, whitewashed room with many books crammed into a small bookcase next to some black, vinyl chairs. "Sit down," he offered me a seat.

The doctor was about 50 years old, gray hair here and there, a prominent chin and blue piercing eyes. His face seemed impartial, I read nothing on it.

"Laura, you're old enough to receive bad news."

I watched him with a mixture of fear and anticipation.

"You know, Laura ... your mom has cancer."

I wanted to say something, but all my words froze on my lips like icicles on the eaves of the house. "Cancer means Death." I associated these two words. There was nothing to say, but still I asked, hoping like a child: "Is it bad?"

"She's in the last stage, my dear. Pray for her not to have terrible pain. Of course, we will give her morphine, but now, in these troubled times, it is tough to get."

At that moment, I couldn't cry. The shock was too much. I mumbled a "thank you, doctor" or something like that. I was the only one who knew at the time. However, I wanted to talk to my dad and cry until exhausted.

*   *   *

I stayed with my mother in the hospital until the Christmas holiday had passed. On December 25th, my mother and I watched on TV, (as did all Romanians,) the shooting of Ceausescu and his wife, at Targoviste. I nurtured a sense of pity for those two old people. During their tyranny, they starved and killed people. I expressed there in the hospital my opinion regarding the killing of Ceausescu family: "It's not a Christian thing to do," I said.

A fat woman who suffered an operation on stomach heckled me: "They killed many people. Let them die! In fact, it's better for everybody that they die!"

I had no one to talk to, so I thought to myself that "no other nation killed its president on a holy day."

Mom moaned slightly. I looked at her, and she looked at me, a sign that her bag needed to be changed. Mother looked good to me. She was on morphine. She no longer needed chemotherapy.

"If the Ceausescus hadn't died so quickly, the terrorists would have killed us," mumbled the old woman who was sharing the same room.

"Yeah, sure," I said. "And who is the enemy?"

During the nights, shots were heard. My father, who was at home (it was a real danger to reach the hospital), said that the terrorists had come into our neighborhood Piper, the district where I lived. My father found out about my mother's illness and he hoped for the best.

"Only God knows," he used to say.

"Yes, Dad, you are right. It is a serious illness that was discovered in the last phase. And maybe she misses Micky too much."

In that period, it seemed like God strengthened me. I had no more tears to cry. But I knew there would come a time when I would cry like a baby and my body would shake.

After the revolutionaries had settled in the country - Romanians had only terrorists in their head - I took my mother home. I did everything in my power to find her morphine because health insurance covered only a certain amount and that was not enough for her pain. Two weeks later, my mother started to have agonizing pain. It was difficult because she was asking questions about her health condition, and we didn't have the right answers. I paid a nurse for eight months to give her morphine. She would groan in agonizing pain less than two hours after her last injection.

She wept bitter tears of pain and I had to be strong for her and comfort her. One day she pulled my collar, and looked me in the eye.

"I want to die, do you understand I want to sleep forever, but this soul … This soul is too stubborn."

I bit my lips till they bled to prevent myself from crying in front of her.

"What is this, Laura, a horrible and cruel joke?"

"Mom, please…"

"Shut up!" she gasped.

After eight months of fierce struggle with cancer, my mother died in my arms on September 6, 1990, calling Micky's name.

* * *

There… we remained lonely, just me and my dad, left in a large house surrounded by quiet painful memories.

Soon I took a job as a coach at Dynamo.The salary was too little, so I quit shortly after I had longed so much for it. I could barely managed to survive with that small a salary and my father's small pension. I had to follow my huge dreams. My dream was dressed in so much light and greatness and I could see it clearly. Somehow I had to touch my dream in this life.

I turned back to the Gymnastics Federation and I asked for help. They offered me a job in northern Italy, 2 hours by car to Venice. I knew that I had to leave my father all alone, but he had a life and I had a dream to catch. The past should be left behind to haunt us, but we knew for sure that nothing would be forgotten. Never. Silent memories were engraved in our hearts.

One day I came home from Federation. Madalina accompanied me. In the dim light of the lamp I saw my father. He was reading with his glasses perched on his nose. Like me, he got so caught up in his book.

"Good evening, Dad," I smiled sadly.

Madalina greeted my father and then she went to him and suddenly snatched the glasses off his nose. Madalina was our wanted guest and our house was her house also.

"Hey guys," my father said gladly.

"Hey," said Madalina. "How are you?"

"When Laura is not here I feel like time drags, so I kill my time reading."

Madalina slightly smiled and looked at me.

"Okay, I'm going to take a shower," she said. "You two have things to discuss."

I was afraid to speak; I knew my dad hated loneliness, which he considered as a kind of intruder. It was early March, but winter still had no desire to leave. It began to snow again and the wind was blowing pretty hard. Dad put some brushwood in the wood stove.

I sat on the couch beside the chair where my father was resting. I moistened my lips, slightly fearful, and then I began to speak weakly. I told my dad that I had been to the Federation and they offered me a coaching job in Sermide, Italy. The crease between his eyebrows deepened harder, like two brown ditches.

"That far, Laura?"

His voice hoarse with emotion softened. I took his hand and I put it lovingly on my cheek.

"Daddy, you will be happy, you'll see…"

He flinched and he pulled back his hand.

"Yes, in loneliness, through the curtains of memories… of pain…"

"No, Dad, you shouldn't think like this. I'll come home twice a year, but I have to follow my dream. I must. At least, I think so now."

Dad hugged me strongly, squeezing me to his chest.

"You're right, Laura, I am not blind to realize that you crave a world that I can't give you."

"No, Dad, it's not that. But if you want me to stay, I will stay here with you. But… you know…there is nothing here for me in the distant future.

"No, darling. You have my blessing to go. You know very well that your happiness is mine."

"Dad," I said wistfully, "where has the time gone? How is it that we just remain?"

"Leave the past to rest, darling. I can't afford to be nostalgic. I'm not allowed. Otherwise, I would grow old much sooner. My soul would groan."

"I'll stay, Dad," I firmly said. "Maybe I'll be able to work somewhere,"

"Work, Laura? Where?"

"Anywhere."

"NO! You are only 21 and life is giving you a chance. Don't waste it. Your father can take care of himself, don't worry."

*   *   *

I coached in Sermide for one year. The nights were cold and hard. I had nightmares that threw me into a darkness, shaking me from my dreams. Mom was dancing in front of me, clad in black, like a ghost and she called me. Then another nightmare, also with my mother, this time she was in a coffin, all purple. She watched me and she wanted to hurt me.

"Why, Mom? Why are you torturing me?"

My heart was racing in my chest ready to break it and I felt like Death was after me with his creepy scythe. I woke up every night sweating and feeling lonely. I would pinch myself to make sure I was still alive.

One morning I talked to my host, an old, pretty nice lady. I had purple circles under my eyes and I felt that all my power and energy had flowed from my body. I couldn't work.

"What is it, Laura?" She asked me. "You seem lost in the darkness."

I sat down beside her. "Nightmares are killing me, Mrs. Leonor. I'm seeing my dead mother, all transfigured. I'm seeing death itself."

My host waved a hand through the air, like a little flag.

"Drop the blackness around you, Laura."

She was a faithful woman who wanted the best for me. I was still dressed in black. I hadn't changed my clothes since coming to Italy.

"Light will bless you if you throw away these ugly clothes."

"But I'm still mourning my mother, madam."

"Your soul mourns, not your clothes."

That day I threw my black clothes in the trash and I bought somemore colorful clothes. After that, my mother smiled in my dreams as an angel from heaven. My nightmares were gone.

I had nightly conversations with my mother, my grandfather and Micky. Each one offered me up a smile.

I bought phone cards almost daily so I could talk to dad everyday.

"Are you are ok, Laura?"

"Yes father, and I will come home soon. I don't know why, but I think I am doing something wrong. I have this sense of loneliness. I paused a moment and then I said: "Dad ... I stopped wearing black. The black clothes I was wearing were disrupting my dreams, my life..."

My father understood. He knew that suffering resides in the soul.

*   *   *

I lef tSermide and movedback home after one year. That city seemed so foreign to me. I earned some money, but it was nowhere near what I had expected.

One year later after returning to Romania, I got married. At the time, Silviu was everything to me. Even so, I didn't cease to think – rarely, but still–of Cosmin Licaciu, the hansome boy of my youth. My first love. I thought of him only with a shadow of nostalgia. The way it could have been ... if we were...

Three years later I gave birth to a boy. I named Dennis Michael. I forgot to mention something important. My godfather at my wedding was my former coach, Stefanescu. Some years later his son, Michael, baptized my baby.

I was happy, although we struggled financially. I wanted more for my child. We were helped by my father, quite often, with his pension, but it still wasn't enough. Dennis Michael became my father's universe. He told me one day that Michael was the reason he lived. Dennis was his reason for his being.

Unfortunately, my marriage only lasted eight years. I continued to work in Italy for 11 years. At 37, I gave birth to a daughter, Emma. Emma is my daughter, all mine. Now I'm happy. I have two beautiful children smiling at me like two flowers in a vase.

And another thing. I got Cosmin.

*   *   *

March of 2011

Winter is slowly creeping to an end. March was full of snow. I went to Romania to solve some personal issues. Dad was traveling with me. I took him to Italy to help me with the children and then back to Romania. Here we are after two years of absence, me, my father and my two beautiful children in Romania.

One evening, when Emma was watching cartoons on TV, I opened my laptop wanting to contact someone on Facebook. Outside it was pitch dark, only some lights brightened the darkness.

I talked to some friends, then, all of a sudden, a bright image of a young man appeared to me as an oasis of peace. Although 23 years had passed, his beautiful smile was still there. His face concealed some fine wrinkles, like spider threads, but the eyes were the same, same light, same brightness.

There he was. My first love. Cosmin.

I felt warm my eyes teared, like that 23 years ago teenager that I was. I didn't know what to do or if I should act in some way. I had heard that he was married and he had two beautiful children. What was the point to enter into his life as an outsider? Maybe he wouldn't want to hear from me again?

But I listened to my heart and I asked permission to talk to him. I eagerly wanted to hear his voice, that voice that bewitched me long time ago. I asked him for his phone number.

In just a few seconds, the numbers began to appear one by one on the screen. I could hardly believed that it was so simple to talk to him after 23 years of absence. It was so simple, so unexpected. Was I crazy? My inner struggles were indescribable.

That night, a quite starless night, I called him. His voice echoed in my ears, rummaging up memories.

"Hey, Laura." Were his first words. I lost myself and I didn't know what to say.

I had a lump in my throat. My feelings, freshly awakened, floated somewhere between me and him on that tiny thread that united us. Even though we were thousands of miles away from each other. Thank God for the internet!

He said he was divorced with two children. A girl and a boy. Quite big, and they were living in Mexico with their mother.

"Are you drowning in loneliness, my love?" ,I wanted to ask.

I hoped for him to be drowning in solitude.

Or: "Are the women still swarming around you like old times?"

Although I hadn't seen him for so many years, I felt again the sting of jealousy.

I didn't say anything like that. I was no longer a teenager.

That night we didn't sleep. We remebered our youth and I tried to not cry filled with so many emotions. My world was suddenly upside down and I didn't know how to react. Was it right what I was doing? Will my conscience let me sleep?

After that night, for another seven months, we talked every night. Shortly after that, Cosmin Licaciu became my husband, and I was by far the happiest woman in the world.

*   *   *

Our first night together.

Moonlight danced over Las Vegas and within us. Finally we had found each other after such a long absence. We made passionate crazy unexpected love.

In the morning, he brought me breakfast in bed in a cheerful happy way. I loved him with all my being, from every part of my soul. I never stopped loving him after all these years. Love burst from every pore of mine.

We ate toast, butter and apricot jam and we drank a lot of coffee with milk. Then he took me by the hand and wrapped in my robe. We went out on the balcony. He took me in his arms and kissed me passionately.

I leaned on him and I looked into the sky.

"Hey," he told me, "I always keep my promises, and you know that, don't you?"

I looked at him smiling, but I didn't understand what he meant.

"I promised that one day we would look together at the sun being in the same place. Married."

I laughed loudly. And then I understood.

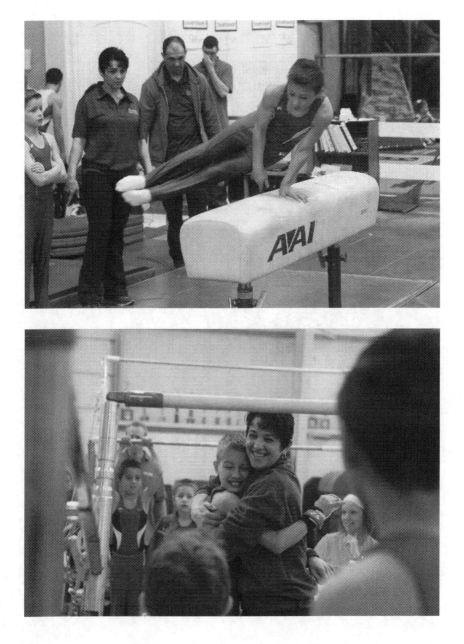